Replenish the Earth:

A Primer in Human Ecology

G. Tyler Miller, Jr.

Professor of Chemistry and Human Ecology

St. Andrews Presbyterian College

Wadsworth Publishing Company, Inc.
Belmont, California

Designer: Gary A. Head

Editor: Katherine Head

Technical Illustrator: John Foster

ISBN-0-534-00203-X

L. C. Cat. Card No. 77-189874

Printed in the United States of America

This book is printed on 100% recycled paper.

5 6 7 8 9 10 — 76 75

Preface

Most of us think of the earth we live on as a spaceship. A major purpose of this book is to show that how most of us think of the almost trite term *spaceship earth* is an arrogant and dangerous reversal of its real meaning. Not only do we misinterpret its meaning, but very few of us have realized or accepted the fundamental limitations and challenges it imposes. Even fewer of us have translated this idea into our patterns of living.

A basic theme of this book is that we must change our worldview from one of arrogance and ever-increasing dominance to humility and cooperation with the magnificent chemical cycles that renew our air, water, and soil. Man's tendency is to order everything — to convert the world into straight lines. Until recently our worldview has been one of ever-increasing linear growth in a world with seemingly inexaustible resources.

Worldview I: Linear Growth and Thinking in an Infinite World

The space program and our increasingly evident ecological crisis have made many of us acutely aware of our finiteness and the fact that we live in a closed system. We have shifted to what might be termed a *pseudo-spaceship* worldview.

Worldview II: Linear Growth and Thinking in a Finite World

But our global ecosystem is not linear. It is a closed cyclical or cybernetic system that tends to maintain a balanced or steady state through an interlocking series of chemical cycles that reuse and replenish the chemicals vital to life. In the long run, in any closed system, continued linear growth and thinking are profoundly disruptive. The message of ecology is that everyone and everything on this planet are interconnected, whether we like it or not, and the goal of ecology is to find out *how* everything is connected. No one can ever completely "do his own thing." Our basic problem, then, is to convert from a linear way of thinking and acting to one based on a cyclical or cybernetic view of nature in which we *replenish the earth and each other.*

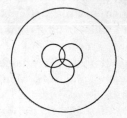

Worldview III: Interdependent Existence in a Cybernetic World — Replenish the Earth

Unfortunately, some of our more prominent environmentalists are offering relatively quick and simple cures by attempting to reduce our complex environmental ills to a single controlling variable such as population, affluence, or the misuse of technology. The emphasis in this book is that our ecological problems and solutions are complex, not simple. Many variables must be dealt with simultaneously, and the idea that there is a quick or simple cure may now be one of the most serious long-range threats to the stability of our global and local ecosystems and to the quality of human life.

There has been a virtual explosion of books on the ecological crisis. Many of these, from which I have borrowed liberally and received numerous insights, are listed in the bibliography at the end of this book. A number of these first-generation books are anthologies of articles providing important insights into our complex ecological problems, but many others have tended to be recitals of ecological facts and horror stories with little or no use of principles to help the reader to understand the problems and possible solutions.

Unless one has an overall ecological worldview in which to interconnect and evaluate these and other sources, it is easy to become confused. This book is meant to provide such a framework by developing some major ecological concepts such as the First and Second Laws of Thermodynamics, the structure of ecosystems, ecosystem function (chemical cycling and energy flow), diversity and stability, and cybernetics, and by applying these concepts to specific ecological problems. This book is a primer: a nontechnical introduction to human ecology for the layman or for college or high-school students taking courses in the sciences, the social sciences, or the humanities. The teacher or student can use this as a base for discussing and applying ecological thinking to his own discipline or interest.

The tone of this book is neither gloom-and-doom pessimism nor rosy technological optimism. Indeed, both of these approaches are death traps for us all: they both lead to "cop-outs," whether fatalism, self-withdrawal, or the naive belief that a fairy god-mother or some technological miracle will save us in the nick of time. My approach is one of hope and cautious optimism that enough of the passengers on our fragile craft can and will become ecologically informed and active before it is too late. In a non-linear cybernetic system efforts can be multiplied or amplified quickly to very high levels through a principle known as synergy. If we can understand and learn to use the positive synergy mechanisms built into our global ecosystem, there are considerable grounds for hope. In this way the ecological movement can move out of its present counterproductive phase of confrontation politics, simplistic thinking, and media overexposure.

I wish to thank all of those who took the time to point out errors and to suggest many improvements. The deficiencies remaining are mine, not theirs. I am particularly indebted to

Professors Edward J. Kormondy, The Evergreen State College, C. S. Holling, The University of British Columbia, Paul P. Feeny, Cornell University, Marion Reeve, Merritt College, Robert A. Richardson, University of Wisconsin, Richard A. Cooley, University of California at Santa Cruz, John C. Williams, College of San Mateo, Richard G. Rose, West Valley College, and my colleague at St. Andrews Presbyterian College, Robert A. Pedigo. Finally, my sincere thanks go to Mrs. Ruth Y. Wetmore for her skill and patience in typing the manuscript and to Jack C. Carey of Wadsworth Publishing Company for knowing how and when to give help and encouragement to an author struggling to give birth to a manuscript.

G. Tyler Miller, Jr.

Contents

Prologue   1

1   The Problem—Around the Bend on a J-Curve   5

   1–1   The Two Most Important Facts of Our Existence 5
   1–2   The Population Bomb 6
   1–3   The Consumption and Pollution Bombs 12
   1–4   Cowboy to Spaceship Rules—More Implications
         of the J-Curve 13

2   A Short Course in Human Population
    Dynamics   16

   2–1   Birth Rates and Death Rates 16
   2–2   Age Structure 17
   2–3   Fertility Rate 24
   2–4   Population Density—The Population Implosion 33
   2–5   What Will Happen?—The S-Curve 35

3   Two Spaceship Laws We Can't Repeal   42

   3–1   Scientific Laws 42
   3–2   You Can't Get Something for Nothing — The First Law of
         Thermodynamics 43
   3–3   If You Think Things Are Mixed Up Now Just Wait — The
         Second Law of Thermodynamics 45
   3–4   Our Arrogant Use of the Term "Spaceship Earth" 51
   3–5   The Environmental Crisis is an Entropy Crisis 54

4 Our Life-Support System 57

4–1 Solar Energy and the Biosphere 57
4–2 Life on Earth Depends on Energy Flow and Chemical
Recycling 59
4–3 What is an Ecosystem? 61
4–4 What Can Go Wrong in an Ecosystem? 66
4–5 The Carbon and Oxygen Cycles 68
4–6 The Nitrogen Cycle 74
4–7 Disrupting the Nitrogen Cycle 75

5 Preserving Stability in Our Life-Support System 83

5–1 A Short Course in Cybernetics 83
5–2 Preserving Ecological Diversity 87
5–3 Ecological Backlash 90
5–4 DDT in Your Fatty Tissue — Biological Magnification 93
5–5 Man Simplifies the Ecosystem 96
5–6 Land-Use Planning 97

6 World Hunger 100

6–1 All Flesh is Grass — Food Chains, Pyramids,
and Webs 100
6–2 Why Most People in the World Can't Eat Steak — Food
Chains and the Second Law of Thermodynamics 104
6–3 World Hunger is Primarily Protein Hunger 105
6–4 Technological Optimists Keep Forgetting About
Thermodynamics 107
6–5 Growing More Food is Not Enough 113

7 Pollution, Technology, and Overpopulation 117

7–1 There Are Two Types of Overpopulation 117
7–2 The Most Overpolluted Country in the World 121
7–3 To Exist is to Pollute — The Law of Conservation
of Pollution 124
7–4 Are We Running Out of Resources? 125
7–5 The First and Second Thermodynamic Revolutions 133
7–6 World Models — Intuitively Obvious Solutions May
Lead to Disaster 134

8 A Case for Hope 145

8–1 Have We Booked Passage on the Titanic? 145
8–2 The Future Depends on the Things We Give Up 147
8–3 All the News Isn't Bad — The People Are Stirring 149

9 What We Must Do! 153

9–1 The Three Levels of Environmental Awareness 153
9–2 A Spaceship-Earth Program 156
9–3 Major Causes of the Environmental Crisis 158
9–4 What We Must Do 160
9–5 What Can You Do? 170

Epilogue 173

Selected Bibliography 175

Index 186

Prologue

Passengers on Terra I, the only true spacecraft, it is time for you to hear the annual state of the spaceship report. As you know, we are hurtling through space at about 66,600 miles per hour on a fixed course. Although we can never return to home base to take on new supplies, our ship has a marvelous and complex life-support system that uses solar energy to recycle the chemicals needed to provide a reasonable number of us with adequate water, air, and food.

There are about 3.7-billion passengers on board, with groups from over 145 countries occupying various sections of the ship. This cultural diversity, along with the diversity of animal and plant life on board, is essential for the long-term ecological stability of our life-support system. Paradoxically, this diversity of human cultures also threatens us. The present lack of trust and cooperation and the continued fighting among some groups can destroy many, if not all, of us. Only about 12 percent of you are American and Russian, but your powerful array of weapons and your ever-increasing use of our finite resources to build more destructive weapons must concern each of us. You have argued that the arms buildup will help us all by insuring peace through mutual deterrence. Some have wondered whether your real purpose is to protect your luxury cabins and services. It is also very distressing to see that some of you are wiping out many of the plant and animal species upon which all of our lives depend.

Let me briefly summarize the state of our passengers and of our life-support system. One quarter of you have occupied the good to luxurious quarters in the tourist and first-class sections. You have used about 70 to 80 percent (some say 90 percent) of all supplies available this past year. Most of the Americans have the most lavish quarters. Even though they represent only about 5½ percent of our total population, they alone used about 40 percent of this year's supplies. They have even returned a small fraction of the ship's resources to some of the 2.8 billion of you travelling in the hold of the ship to help you increase your standard of living. However, with the finite supplies and recycling capacity of our craft, many of you are now questioning whether or not there are enough resources for a significant number to ever move from the hold to the tourist and first-class sections, in spite of glowing technological assurances from your paternalistic American friends. And even more important, many of you are asking why you have to travel in the hold of the ship.

I am saddened to say that things have not really improved this year for the 75 percent of our passengers travelling in the hold. Over two-thirds of you are suffering from hunger, malnutrition, or both, and three-fourths of you do not have adequate water or shelter. More people died from starvation and malnutrition this year than at any time in the history of our voyage. This number will certainly rise as long as your soaring population growth wipes out any small gains in food supply and economic development. Recently the American passengers have provided some of you with a means for increasing food yields. This so-called "green revolution" may temporarily keep your famine and misery rate from rising and buy a little time for you to control population growth. Even this agricultural breakthrough may be a limited blessing because of its disastrous side effects on oversimplifying and polluting our life-support system.

Although the records are not clear, it is believed that our voyage began several million years ago with only two passengers. A plot of the length in time of our voyage versus the increase in passengers from the original two passengers to the 3.7 billion now on board, yields a curve in the shape of the letter "J." The most important fact molding our lives today is that we have gone around the bend on a J-curve of increasing population and pollution. At the present rate, our population will double to over 7 billion passengers in the next 35 years.

No one knows the maximum number of persons our ship's

supplies and recycling systems can support. Some of our engineers say the upper limit is 10- to 15-billion passengers — a number we could reach in only 40 to 50 years. One highly optimistic engineer believes we could support 30-billion passengers. Unfortunately, these estimates are for maximum levels, with almost everyone living in misery just barely above the starvation level. The more important question is, what is the optimum population and consumption level that will allow all passengers to have a quality life involving freedom, dignity, and a fair share of our finite resources? Some experts estimate this figure to be about 1- to 2-billion passengers, a figure we surpassed long ago.

But population growth in the hold of the ship is only part of the problem. The hold is overpopulated in relation to available food. In the past few years, we have recognized a second type of overpopulation that is even more serious because it threatens our entire life-support system. This type of overpopulation is occurring in the tourist and first-class sections. It is not a problem of a lack of food or space, but one of overpopulation relative to the level of consumption and the resulting pollution of our environment. Two additional J-curves of increasing consumption and pollution rise sharply with even a slight growth in population in the tourist and first-class cabins. The 207-million Americans used 40 percent of all of our supplies and produced about 50 percent of our man-made pollution during the past year. Each American tourist and first-class passenger has about 25 to 50 times the impact on the life-support system as each passenger travelling in the hold. In this sense, the American section is the most overpopulated one on the ship. The Americans and other passengers travelling tourist or first class must reduce their population and simultaneously reduce and redirect their wasteful patterns of consumption that squander much of our limited supplies. Failure to do this may disrupt, or impair, our life-support system beginning in the first-class cabins.

We are now passing through the early stages of our first major spaceship crisis, an interlocking crisis of overpopulation, pollution, resource depletion, and the danger of mass destruction by intergroup warfare. Some have expressed the fear that the ship is already doomed, while other technological optimists project a glorious future for everyone. Our most thoughtful experts agree that the situation on this ship is most serious, but certainly not hopeless. They feel that if we begin now, we have about 30 to 50 years to learn how to control our population and consumption and to learn how to live together in cooperation and peace on this beautiful and fragile lifecraft that is our home. Obviously, this means that a far greater number of us must begin to act like crewmen rather than passengers, particularly those of you travelling tourist or first-class who have the greatest negative impact on our environment and who have the greatest resources to correct the situation.

Just what is spaceship Terra I? Where are we going? What is the nature of the problems we face? What is our individual responsibility for the other passengers and for preserving our life-support system? Let us begin to look more deeply into these complex questions so that we may then convert our understanding into effective individual and group action.

The Problem — Around the Bend on a J-Curve

1–1 The Two Most Important Facts of Our Existence

Spaceship Terra I is obviously the earth.[1] Consequently, the two most important facts of our global existence are·

---

1. We all live on a spaceship, a closed system of finite size and resources.
2. Our life-support system is threatened because we have gone around the bend on a J-curve of increasing population, use of resources, and pollution.

We seemingly live in the midst of a crisis of crises.[2] Something has gone wrong during the past few decades. Increased control over nature is not producing safety and peace of mind. As we grow richer materially, our environment grows poorer. As some acquire more leisure, they find less available space and beauty to

---

[1] All population figures and percentages in the prologue are based on the 1971 World Population Data Sheet, Population Reference Bureau, Inc., Washington, D.C., August, 1971.

[2] For a listing of our planetary problems in order of their importance, with estimates of time to disaster for each problem, and a summary of what we must do, see the superb article entitled "What We Must Do" by J. R. Platt, *Science*, *116*, 1115 (1969).

enjoy. Technological innovations create problems which require even bigger and more expensive counter technologies to correct their impact on the environment.

Regardless of what we do or where we go, we can no longer escape the symptoms of our ecological crisis; our senses are bombarded with constant reminders. You can feel it in the tremor of anxiety that runs through our society, in the increasing unrest, frustration, and alienation, in the deterioration of public services, and in the progressive loss of privacy and freedom. You can smell it in our choking air and rotting rivers, lakes, and oceans.

Those predicting the end of man or of the world are premature. However, spaceship earth is definitely in trouble. Many are starving now and the casualties will surely increase. Maintaining or increasing the quality of life will be a formidable task. Let us begin by looking at the number and condition of the passengers on spaceship earth.

1–2 The Population Bomb

What is a J-curve and what does it mean to say that "we have gone around the bend on a J-curve?" Any system that grows by doubling, that is, 1, 2, 4, 8, 16, 32, . . . is involved in geometric, or exponential, growth. A plot of the change in size of the numbers after a series of doublings or after various lengths of time, yields a curve in the shape of the letter "J." For a long time nothing much appears to happen. Then suddenly there is a catastrophic change in the size of the numbers as the bend in the "J" is rounded and the curve heads almost straight up.

Let me take you around the bend on a J-curve, using a very simple example. Let us double a page of this book over and over again and note the total thickness after each doubling. Assuming that the page has a thickness of about 0.1 millimeter (about 1/254 of an inch), then after the first doubling the thickness would be 0.2 millimeters, then 0.4, 0.8, 1.6, 3.2, and so on. After eight doublings the paper would be 25.6 millimeters, or approximately 1 inch in thickness. Nothing much has happened. After 12 doublings it would be slightly over 1 foot in thickness and after 20 doublings, 340 feet in thickness. Still very little has happened, we are on the lower part, or lag phase, of the J-curve.

Now let us go around the bend. If we could physically double this page only 35 times (actually about 35½), its approximate thickness would reach from New York to Los Angeles, some 3000 miles. Something almost incomprehensible happened as we went around the bend of the "J." Once around the bend and heading straight up, as shown in Figure 1-1, the shock becomes even greater. If we could double this page only about 42 times, it would reach from the earth to the moon, some 240,000 miles, and doubling it slightly over 50 times would give a thickness reaching from here to the sun, some 93-million miles.[3] What happens with exponential growth is that eventually the ever-growing base builds to such a large number that each future doubling represents an astronomical increase in the total.

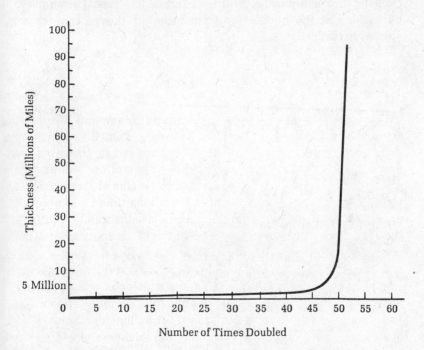

Figure 1–1 The exponential, or J-curve, growth in thickness as a page in this book is doubled successively.

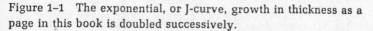

[3] You only need to be able to multiply by two to verify these calculations. Also see Footnote on pages 36 and 37.

Is this just playing games with numbers with no application to the real world? Unfortunately, this sort of J-curve also applies to the present growth of the human population on earth, as shown in Figure 1-2.

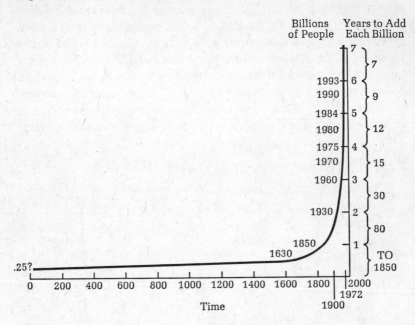

Figure 1–2 J-curve of world's population growth past and projected (if present rate of growth continues).

You can see that we have rounded the bend and are now heading almost straight up.

Professor Paul Ehrlich of Stanford University has called our present population growth a "population bomb," [4] the most deadly explosion in the history of mankind. Let's listen to this explosion.

Consider a metronome ticking away. The net birth rate [5] on

---

[4] P. R. Ehrlich, *The Population Bomb*, Ballantine Books, 1968.

[5] Birth and death rates can be expressed in several different ways. In this case I am using the net birth or death rate, that is, the total number of human beings born or dying per day or year. Demographers — people who make a profession of studying human population — normally use the *crude* birth or death rate. It is defined as the number of births or deaths per thousand people in a population per year.

this planet is now approximately 232 persons (ticks) per minute or approximately 334,000 per day, while the net death rate is ticking at about 93 persons per minute or approximately 134,000 per day. In other words, the birth rate is over two times the death rate. Population growth is not determined by birth rate (BR) or death rate (DR) but by the difference between the two (BR-DR). This means that we are now adding about 200,000 additional passengers each day, or 1.4 million each week, or 70 million each year.[6] This difference between the birth rate and death rate is the "population bomb."

The Population Bomb

Net birth rate (BR)	= 334,000 per day
Net death rate (DR)	= 134,000 per day
Population increase (BR – DR)	= 200,000 per day
	= 1.4 million per week
	= 70 million per year

This is an annual increase equivalent to the entire population of the planet 4000 years ago. It means adding the equivalent of the entire U.S. population every three years. It means adding the food, shelter, and resources for the equivalent of a city of 1.4-million people every single week without stop, at a time when we can't even make most of our existing cities decent places to live much less build new ones every week. In the past 24 hours India alone increased by 40,000 and the United States added 6,000 people and 12,000 automobiles.

All of these new passengers must be fed, clothed, and housed; each will use a portion of our finite resources and add to our global pollution. While this overwhelming addition of new passengers is occurring, the United Nations estimates that one-half to two-thirds of our present passengers are either hungry or malnour-

---

[6] These and the remaining population figures in this section are based on the 1971 World Population Data Sheet. Population Reference Bureau, Inc., Washington, D.C., August, 1971.

ished, and three out of four don't have adequate housing and are without a safe and adequate water supply.[7] There are more hungry and weakened people on this planet now than there were human beings in 1850.

It is difficult to comprehend the catastrophic change in population that has occurred on our tiny ship during only the past few decades. We glibly speak of millions and billions of people without realizing what this means.

One way of describing exponential change is in terms of doubling time, that is, the time (usually in years) that it takes for a population to double in size. The doubling time of the human population has decreased from the 1650 years between the time of Christ and the middle of the seventeenth century to only 35 years at present growth rates, as shown in Table 1-1. Perhaps the major

Table 1-1   Doubling times for the human population.*

Date	Estimated World Population	Doubling Time
0 A.D.	250 million	
1650 A.D.	500 million	1,650 years
1850 A.D.	1 billion	200 years
1930 A.D.	2 billion	80 years
1975 A.D.	4 billion	45 years
2010 A.D.	8 billion?	35 years
2040 A.D.	16 billion?	30 years

*Keyfitz, Nathan. "How Many People Have Ever Lived on Earth?" *Population Bulletin,* vol. 18, no. 1. Population Reference Bureau, 1962.

significance of this statistic is that with each doubling of the population, much of the life-support system of the spaceship must also double if the quality of life is to be maintained; we would need twice as many hospitals, schools, bushels of wheat, highways, kilowatts of energy, and so on.

Thus, in human-population growth not only is the base of people increasing sharply but the time rate of increase is also accelerating, as shown by the steady decrease in the doubling time.

---

[7] John McHale, *The Ecological Context,* George Braziller, Inc., 1970, p. 13.

This means that, technically speaking, the term "population bomb" is far too mild a term to describe our population growth. After a bomb has gone off the force of the explosion steadily decreases with time and distance from the explosion site. Human population growth on the other hand is getting larger and growing even faster as time goes on. It is more analogous to a runaway chain reaction in a nuclear reactor. The questions we must determine are what is the human critical mass and how do we prevent our population from attaining this critical mass?

Another way of understanding our predicament is to look at the time it takes to replace passengers lost by the traditional death-rate increases due to war, famine, or disease, as shown in Table 1-2.

Table 1–2 Some implications of going around the bend on a J-curve.*

Some Past Disasters	Approximate Number killed	Present world population growth replaces the equivalent of this loss in approximately
Pakistan tidal wave, 1970	200,000	1 day
All Americans in all our wars	600,000	3 days
Great flood, Hwang-Lo River, 1887	900,000	4½ days
Famine in India, 1769-1770	3,000,000	2 weeks
China famine, 1877-78	9,500,000	7 weeks
Present global famine	15,000,000/ year	2½ months
All wars in the past 500 years (some 250 wars)	35,000,000	6 months
Bubonic plague (Black Death), 1347-1351	75,000,000	13 months

*Casualty figures obtained from *The World Almanac* — 1971, Newspaper Enterprise Associates, New York, p. 807, and *Information Please Almanac* — 1970, Dan Golenpaul Associates, New York, p. 794.

It seems incredible that at our present population increase of approximately 200,000 per day, it takes *only three days* to replace in numbers all Americans killed in all of our wars, and only *six months to replace all of the battlefield casualties in all of man-*

kind's 250 wars during the past 500 years. The largest single disaster in the history of mankind, the Bubonic plague, claimed over
75-million lives. It now takes only 13 months to replace this many
people.

1-3   The Consumption and Pollution Bombs

Unfortunately, there are other J-curves that we must contend
with, particularly in our affluent nation. The major growth in industrialization in the United States has occurred since 1946, following World War II. Between 1946 and 1968 the U.S. population
increased by about 43 percent while our GNP per capita increased
by about 59 percent.[8] Barry Commoner[9] has shown that during

Table 1-3   Rise in per captia consumption of environmentally harmful
items in the United States between 1946 and 1968.

Item	Percent Increase in Consumption Per Capita
Mercury	2,150
Synthetic fibers	1,792
Plastics	1,024
Nitrogen fertilizer	534
Synthetic organic chemicals	495
Aluminum	317
Detergents	300
Electric power	276
Pesticides	217
Wood pulp	152
Motor vehicles	110
Cement	74
GNP (per capita)	59

During this same period U.S. population increased by 43 percent.

[8] *Statistical Abstract of the U.S. 1970,* U.S. Department of Commerce,
p. 5 and *The National Income and Productivity Accounts of the United
States, 1929-65,* U.S. Department of Commerce, p. 4-5.
[9] Based on figures in Commoner, B., Corr, M., and Stamler, P.S.,
"The Causes of Pollution," *Environment, 13,* 2-19 (1971).

this same 22-year period the per capita consumption or production of environmentally harmful items has increased from 74 to over 2000 percent, as shown in Table 1-3.

Obviously these increases do not all end up as pollutants in the environment, but they have resulted in a significant increase in pollution.

What may happen in the future as we progress further up the J-curves of increasing consumption and pollution? The U.S. population is growing at a rate of approximately 1 percent per year — doubling about every 63 years. But the annual growth rate of our industrial production is around 4 percent — doubling about every 17 years. This means that if we continue on our present course, then in 63 years our effect on the world environment would be about 12 times greater than it is now. We would have to improve pollution control about 1200 percent in the next 63 years just to maintain our present unacceptable environmental conditions.[10]

1–4 Cowboy to Spaceship Rules — More Implications of the J-Curve

What does it mean to go around the bend on a J-curve if you live on a spaceship? We have only recently become aware of the problem; its profound implications are still matters of some conjecture. What we are beginning to perceive is that our situation will require a radically new set of survival rules. It is as if we had been brought up to learn and perfect the rules for baseball only to find that our survival now depends on finding and learning new rules for a different and much faster game. As the economist Kenneth Boulding[11] put it, we have been living by "cowboy, or frontier, rules," and we must now discover and convert to "spaceship rules."

We have envisioned the earth as a place of unlimited frontiers and resources, where ever-increasing consumption and production inevitably lead to a better life, and where success is measured by Gross National Product rather than Gross National Quality. If

---

[10] F. H. Borman, "Diminishing Man," *Ecology Today,* March, 1971, p. 55.

[11] Kenneth E. Boulding, "The Economics of the Coming Spaceship Earth," from *Environmental Quality in a Growing Economy,* Henry Jarrett (ed), Johns Hopkins Press, 1966.

we polluted or destroyed one area, we merely moved on to another unspoiled area. Now there are no frontiers left, and we must go back and repair some of the damage we have done to our home. We in the developed countries have discovered that more goods do not necessarily bring more happiness and that, in terms of spaceship living, we may be overdeveloped. "Progress American style" each year means over 200-million junked cars, 30-million tons of paper, 76-billion tons of disposable containers, and billions of tons of human, animal, and industrial wastes that are now filling up the aisles on our spacecraft, particularly in our own cabins.[12]

One significant aspect of our problem is the shrinkage of the <u>time factor</u>. Several generations ago, when we were on the lower part of the curve, the world seemed enormous, and man's problems, although serious, appeared to be manageable. There were hundreds of years available to absorb a new idea or technological invention. Because of the relatively small number of people, the impact of new ideas or inventions on the environment was not serious. "Frontier" rules that encouraged individual initiative and competition seemed to produce good social and economic results. But now that the bend of the "J" has been rounded, it seems as though the globe has shrunk; our problems appear endless and the time factor for dealing with them has diminished to a few years, so that in Alvin Toffler's terms we experience "future shock."[13] In fact, we have not just one J-curve but a whole series of them, that is, increasing air pollution, GNP, cars, highways, electrical power, solid waste, emphysema, books on the ecological crisis, and committees to study how to clean the environment. All of these (and many others) are interacting in a complex and for the most part an unknown manner to affect the quality of our lives.

Many are now recognizing that to hold to "frontier rules" will assure a steady decrease in the quality of our lives. We don't know yet the nature of our new spaceship rules, much less how to change some of our present political, economic, technological, and ethical rules or systems to new ones. To bring about such changes

---

[12] U.S. Department of Commerce, *Statistical Abstract of the United States — 1971*, U.S. Government Printing Office, Washington, D.C.

[13] Alvin Toffler, *Future Shock*, Random House, 1970.

14

we must first gain some understanding of how we got ourselves into this predicament.

What is the use of a house if you haven't a decent planet to put it on?

Thoreau

2

A Short Course in Human Population Dynamics

2-1   Birth Rates and Death Rates.

Worldwide birth rates have remained about the same for the past 200 years, with a slight decline during the past 50 years, as shown in Figure 2-1. How then can we possibly have the population explosion that is now occurring?

This is a good example of *population trap number one* that many laymen and newspaper writers and editors continually fall into. *To make predictions about population growth or decline you do not look only at the birth rate.* The birth rate is obviously a factor but it is not the only factor. We must also consider the death rate.

Net population growth or decline over a given time period is not due to birth rate (BR) or death rate (DR), but is the difference between the birth rate and death rate (BR — DR) — the number of passengers being added minus the number of passengers dying during the same time period. Actually, for a given country or region the net-population change is the net birth rate minus the net death rate [1] plus the net migration in or out. Obviously, for the planet as a whole, migration in or out is not a factor.

During the early 1940's two powerful antibiotics, penicillin and streptomycin, and an insecticide called dichlorodiphenyltrichloro-

---

[1] Demographers call this difference between net birth rate and net death rate the natural increase.

Population change per unit time (PC) =

Birth rate (BR) — Death rate (DR) + net migration (M)

or

Country or region: PC = BR — DR + M

Planet: PC = BR — DR

---

ethane, or DDT, were introduced. Since then the world has not been the same. The worldwide use of these and other forms of modern medicine and sanitation have brought about a dramatic decrease in the death rate in developed and underdeveloped countries, as shown in Figure 2-1. As a result, the birth rate for our planet is now over twice as high as the death rate. The important thing to remember is that regardless of the relative values *as long as the birth rate is greater than the death rate over a given time period there will always be a net growth in population.*

Figure 2-2 shows the birth-rate and death-rate curves for the world between 1940 and 1971. During this period the crude birth rate declined slightly from about 36 to 34 births per thousand per year while the crude death rate was cut drastically from about 30 to 14 deaths per thousand per year. The difference between these two curves leads to the J-curve of population growth, as shown earlier in Figure 1-2.

This imbalance between birth rate and death rate explains our present situation, but what about the future population change?[2]

2–2   Age Structure

Let's look at population growth in the United States. In 1970 and 1971 there was a wave of newspaper headlines and editorials declaring "U.S. Population Explosion Over," "Birth Rates At All-Time Low," "Prophets of Doom Wrong Again." Since such

---

[2] For an excellent and more detailed summary of world population growth see "Man's Population Predicament," *Population Bulletin*, Vol. 27, No. 2, Population Reference Bureau (April, 1971).

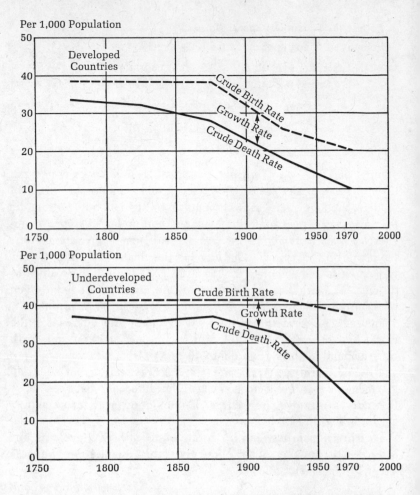

Figure 2–1   Estimated crude birth and death rates in developed and under-developed countries between 1770 and 1970. The difference between the two curves represents population growth in each region. (Source: United Nations, *A Concise Summary of the World Population Situation in 1970*. New York: United Nations, 1971.)

dangerous and misleading stories will probably appear again and again in your lifetime, let us examine their validity.

Fortunately, the U.S. crude birth rate has declined from a high of 26.6 births per thousand per year in 1947 to a low of 17.5 in 1968, but in 1969 it rose slightly to 17.7, it increased to 18.2 in

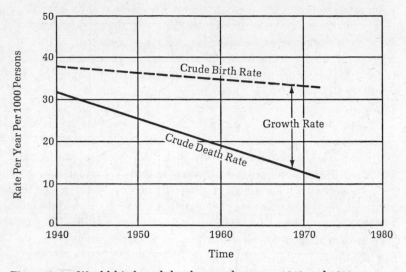

Figure 2–2   World birth and death rates between 1940 and 1970.
(Source: U. N. Demographic yearbooks and Population Reference
Bureau annual data sheets.)

1970 and fell to a new low of 17.3 in 1971.[3] During this same period
the crude death rate has remained almost constant around 9.5 to
9.7 deaths per thousand per year.

Many reporters and editors fell into the classic birth-rate trap
just discussed. Although the rate of our population growth has
declined in recent years, our population has continually increased
simply because we still have almost twice as many births as
deaths per year plus a net immigration of about 400,000 persons
per year.[4] We now have a population of about 209 million, and
every day in the United States an average of about 10,000 babies
are born, about 5,000 persons die, and over 1,000 more persons
immigrate than leave. This adds up to a net increase of about
6,000 a day or 2 million per year or 60 million every 30 years.

But assuming a stable death rate, coupled with the decline in

---

[3] "Annual Summary of Vital Statistics for the United States, 1970,"
U.S. Department of Health, Education, and Welfare and "Population
Profile," Population Reference Bureau, 1967.

[4] At present rates immigration accounts for about 20 percent of U.S.
population growth each year.

birth rate between 1958 and 1972, shouldn't we expect a growth or less than 60-million Americans in the next 30 years? The U.S. Census Bureau predicts an almost certain increase of 75- to 80-million more Americans between now and the year 2000. If people believe these recurring examples of irresponsible reporting, we could easily add 100-million more persons to the American population.

In the next 10 to 20 years it is probable (hopefully) that most Americans will have fewer children per family, but in spite of this our birth rate will almost surely rise. Why? Here uninformed writers fall into *population trap number two*. We must also consider a second factor in population dynamics, that is, *the age structure of the population*. The birth rate for a given time span depends not only on how many babies each woman has, but also on the percentage of women in the prime child-bearing years of ages 20 to 29.

After World War II the soldiers came home and immediately we had a baby boom with high birth rates prevailing from 1947 to 1957. Those babies have grown into women who have moved or will be moving into their peak reproductive years. Women born in 1947 moved into their peak reproductive years in 1967 and will remain there until 1977 while those born in 1957 will move into this phase in 1977 and remain there until 1987. Thus, population trends build up momentum lasting for 20 to 40 years. The high birth rate of the post-war baby boom 20 years ago becomes the potential "mother boom" of the 1970's. Between 1960 and 1980 the number of women in the United States between the ages of 20 and 29 [5] will *almost double,* from 11 million to 20 million, as shown in Figure 2-3. (Any change in present and future birth rates one way or another will not affect this fact, assuming a constant death rate. This represents women already here.)

Thus, our birth rate will probably go up between 1970 and 1980 not because women will have more babies, but primarily because more women will have babies. If we cut the average number of children per family by one-third, for example from 3 to 2, and at the same time double the number of couples, the birth rate will still go up.

---

[5] The total reproductive years normally occur between ages 15 and 44, but the prime reproductive years are from 20 to 29.

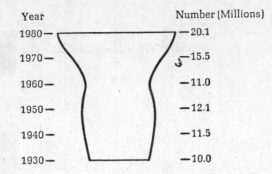

Year	Number (Millions)
1980 —	—20.1
1970 —	—15.5
1960 —	—11.0
1950 —	—12.1
1940 —	—11.5
1930 —	—10.0

Figure 2–3   Number of U.S. women in peak reproductive years (ages 20-29) between 1930 and 1980. (Source: "People," Population Reference Bureau, May, 1970.)

Birth rate minus death rate plus migration determines the population change at a given moment, but the age structure of a population is one of the critical factors determining future population change. We can obtain an age structure diagram for the world or for a given country by plotting the percentages of the total population in three age categories: preproductive (ages 0 to 14), reproductive (ages 15 to 44 with prime reproductive ages 20 to 29), and postreproductive (ages 45 to 75), as shown in Figure 2-4. The percentage of males is shown to the left and the percentage of females to the right of the center line.

The shape of the age structure pyramid is a key to whether a population might expand, decline, or remain stationary. A rapidly expanding population would have a very broad base with a large number already in the productive category and an even larger percentage of young ready to move into this category over the next 15 years. A declining population would have a small base, and a stable population with zero growth rate would form a symmetrical pyramid.

Probably one of the most alarming facts that a person can state is that approximately 37 percent of the people now on this planet are under 15 years of age. In the underdeveloped countries the average is around 42 percent while in the developed countries it is around 28 percent, as summarized in Table 2-1. These young people are the broad base of the world age structure and represent the even greater explosion of population that is to come.

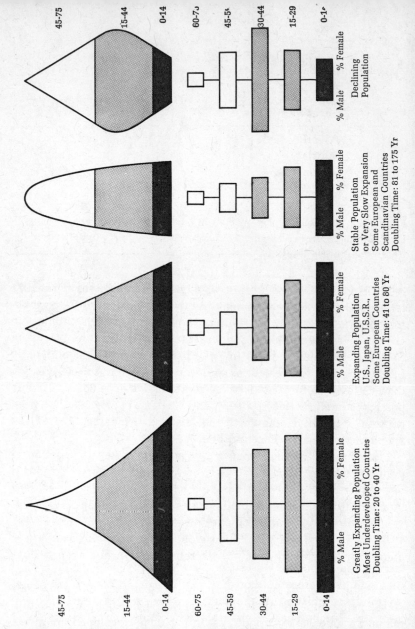

Figure 2–4 Major types of age-structure diagrams for human populations. Dark portions represent preproductive periods (0-14); shaded portions represent reproductive years (15-44); and clear portions are postproductive years (45-75).

Table 2–1   Percent of population under 15 years of age in various regions of the world. (Source: 1971 World Population Data Sheet, August, 1971, Population Reference Bureau, Washington, D.C.)

Region or Country	Percent of Population under 15 Years of Age in 1971
World	37
Africa	45
Latin America	42
Asia	40
U. S.	30
U.S.S.R.	28
Europe	25

Consider the effect of age structure on India, where in 1971 41 percent of its population was under 15 years of age. The population problems of India stagger the imagination. Her population is already over one-half billion, that is, one-seventh of all the world's inhabitants. India has 300 different languages, six major social classes, hundreds of castes, thousands of subcastes, 11 major religions, and nine major political parties.

India is one of the very few countries in the world to have an official population control policy. In fact, it started population control back in 1951 when its population was less than 400 million. What has happened? In only 20 years its population has soared from 400 million to about 570 million in 1971. With its present doubling time of only 27 years it may have around 1.2-billion people (a number equal to about one-third of the present population of the world) by the year 2000. To create enough jobs and industry for its present population would require that India use *all* of its GNP for this purpose only during the next 20 years and during that same time its population may almost double, putting them further behind than before. Although many Indian officials seem to be eternally optimistic that they can slow the growth rate down, we can see that population growth momentum from a broad-based age structure is one of the most powerful forces on this planet.

Indeed, most countries (including the United States) have no official population control policies. Most political leaders, even if they are aware of the implications of destructive population growth, ignore it because it is a politically sensitive issue. Some blindly encourage growth. The president of Mexico ran for office on a platform of promising to encourage population growth in spite of the fact that Mexico has one of the fastest growing populations in the entire world — it doubles every 21 years — and in spite of the fact that most of its people already live in abject poverty. (It has been speculated that by the year 2010 a new "Berlin wall" may be erected between Mexico and the United States in order to prevent population spillover by a starving and disease-ridden Mexican population, four times its present size.)

2–3 Fertility Rate

We have seen the importance of two factors — birth rate minus death rate and the age structure of a population — in determining future population growth or decline. Yet most professional population experts have consistently *underestimated* world population growth in this century [6] — although their estimates are getting closer to reality. Why have the demographers been wrong?

Although the answer is complex and sometimes includes a lack of reliable data, the primary reason lies in the unpredictability of our individual human behavior in deciding how many children constitute an ideal family throughout the 30-year period of the woman's fertility. We must consider a third factor in population dynamics, namely, *fertility rate, or the average number of children a woman has in her reproductive years between 15 and 45.*[7] Thus, even though an unfavorable age structure results in more potential mothers, the rate of population growth can be slowed down if each couple on the average has fewer children per family. If there is a drastic cut in average family size, a population can even level off over a 30-year period. At the same time a slight shift upward in the fertility rate can bring about a catastrophic rise in population.

In the underdeveloped world there are an average of five to six

---

[6] Philip M. Hauser, Director of the University of Chicago Population Research Center, has said that anyone who claims to be able to predict future population change is either a fool or a charlatan.

[7] I am using the total fertility rate. Demographers frequently use the general fertility rate, that is, the number of births per year per thousand women per year in the reproductive ages from 15 to 44.

children per family, while in the developed countries the average is around three children per family. Let's assume (optimistically) that the low death rates continue. Then, in order for world population to eventually stop growing, all families in the world would have to move to an average of 2.11 children per family; that is, each couple would replace itself. (The 0.11 is needed for replacement due to accidents and other unexpected forms of attrition.) Even if this most unlikely event occurred tomorrow, the momentum from our present youthful age structure would mean that we would add over 1-billion more passengers and the world population would not level off for 70 years at around 5 billion, assuming no rise in death rates.

If this replacement-size family of 2.11 children is not reached for the entire world until the year 2000 (still a very unlikely event), the population at that time will be about 5.8 billion. Due to the resulting age structure it would still grow for another 100 years, reaching about 8.2 billion in the year 3000. A possibility closer to reality is that the developed countries could reach an average family size of 2.11 by 2000 with the underdeveloped countries reaching this average fertility by the year 2040. If this happened world population would continue to grow for 100 years until 2140 and then stabilize around 15.5 billion, well over four times our present size.[8] (All of these projections assume that death rates will not rise.)

Again we see clearly that with an unfavorable age structure, the average number of children per couple must be reduced sharply in order to reach population equilibrium within a 30 to 70 year period. Like a passenger on a jet we no longer have the option of getting off at a stop 100 miles down the road. Once around the bend on a J-curve, any country that hopes to level off its population (except by increased death rate) must plan and execute effective population control policies 30 to 70 years ahead. As mentioned earlier, only a handful of countries have any sort of population policy and most of those are either ineffective or designed to increase population. In 1971 the National Academy of Sciences report, *Rapid Population Growth* (Johns Hopkins Press), stated:

---

[8] Figures taken from an address, "Business-Population and the Human Environment," given on February 24, 1971 by Bernard Berelson, President of the Population Council.

'Over a billion births must be prevented in 30 years to get population growth down from 2 to 1 percent by 2000. The task may well be the most difficult mankind has ever faced."

There are some glimmerings of hope that the United States may be moving toward a population policy. In 1970, President Nixon appointed a Commission on Population Growth and the American Future. Their interim report in March, 1971 was encouraging.[9] More important, of course, is whether their recommendations, like those of most presidential commissions, merely become another piece of solid waste buried in government filing cabinets.

More and more Americans are finding that they can't afford the cost of raising many children. Garrett Hardin [10] estimates that the cost of raising one child to age 18 is approximately 2½ times the average income of the family, as summarized in Table 2-2. This cost does not include the cost of college education. To put it another way, *the cost of raising one child to age 18 is roughly*

Table 2–2   The cost of having children in the United States.

Average Annual Family Income	Cost to Raise One Child to Age 18
$ 4,000	$10,000
$ 8,000	$20,000
$12,000	$30,000
$16,000	$40,000
$20,000	$50,000

equivalent to purchasing a home. How many homes can you afford?

Hopefully, more Americans are also realizing that it is the quality of parenthood not the quantity that is important. There are individuals who have the ability to provide a quality parenthood to a large number of children, but such persons are probably rare.

[9] Copies of the interim report and the final report (Spring, 1972) may be obtained from Commission on Population Growth and the American Future, 726 Jackson Place, N.W., Washington, D.C. 20506.

[10] Hardin, G., *Birth Control,* New York: Pegasus, 1970, pp. 26–29.

Why do people have children? Is it to prove their masculinity or femininity? To connect themselves to the future? To provide social status? To provide old-age economic security? To add novelty and fun to a household? To save a marriage? To have power and influence over another person? The answers for a given couple are varied and complex. Indeed, we know very little about why people have children and serious research on the psychology of childbearing is in its infancy.[11]

How close are we to zero population growth in the United States? Let's look briefly at U.S. fertility patterns. During the 1950's and most of the 60's the average American family consisted of around three children, resulting in our present potential "mother boom." Fortunately, the number of children per U.S. family has fallen to about 2.3 in 1971 — but we still have a long way to go to achieve equilibrium, as shown in Table 2-3.

Table 2–3   Changes in U.S. total fertility rates.*

	Annual Averages		Five-Year Averages
1971	2.3	1960-64	3.4
1970	2.5	1955-59	3.7
1969	2.4	1950-54	3.3
1968	2.5	1945-49	3.0
1967	2.6	1940-44	2.5
1966	2.7	1935-39	2.2
1965	2.9	1930-34	2.4

*The average number of children expected of a woman in her years between 14 and 45, as based on current childbirth statistics.

Source: U.S. Census Bureau

If this fertility rate of 2.3 continues, our population would add another 100 million by 2010 and would double by 2040, as shown in Table 2-4.

[11] For a review see Fawcett, J. T., "Psychology and Childbearing," PRB Selection No. 39, Population Reference Bureau, September, 1971.

Table 2–4   U.S. Population projections.*

Average Children Per Woman	1972	1980	1990	2000	2020
			in millions		
3.10	209	237	279	322	447
2.78	209	234	270	305	397
2.45	209	231	261	288	351
2.11	209	228	251	271	307
2.11 and no immigration	209	223	242	256	280

*Source: U.S. Census Bureau

In 1971 the U.S. Bureau of Census projected that if every U.S. couple, beginning tomorrow, just replaced itself with an average of 2.11 children, our population would still grow for the next 70 years and eventually level off at about 300 million. (If the annual immigration of 400,000 was eliminated, our population would level off in about 60 to 70 years, around 2037, with about 285 million Americans.) If we don't achieve the 2.11 child average until 1980 and present immigration rates continue, then our population would level off at about 310 million sometime after 2045. If this replacement average is not reached until 2000, population growth would stop around 2065 with a population of over 400 million. If the present younger generation (0 to 29 years) should return to a three-child family in the 70's and 80's, our population would soar to 300 million by 1996, 400 million by 2014, and 800 million by 2050, four times our present size. Figures 2-5 and 2-6 show the effect of two and three-child families on future U.S. population.

Some concerned citizens are calling for an immediate halt in U.S. population growth. To reach zero population growth in only 10 to 20 years would require that each couple — beginning tomorrow — have an average of only about one child and that we halt our annual immigration of 400,000 persons. (It has been argued that immigration should be slowed down, since much of it involves the United States in draining off perhaps the most valuable resource of underdeveloped countries, namely, brain power.) Thereafter, a constant population level could be maintained if the one-child generation had two children, their grandchildren

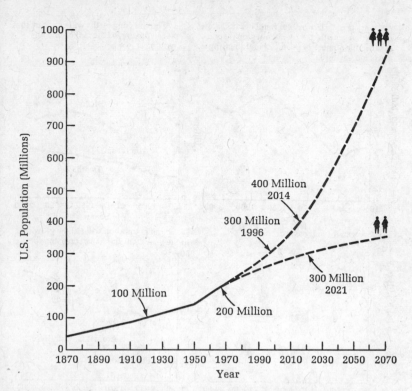

Figure 2–5 The effect of the two-child and three-child family size on U.S. population growth. (Source: Interim report of the Commission on Population Growth and the American future, March, 1971.[12])

returned again to a three-child average, followed by the next generation returning to a one-child family. This accordion-like mechanism would have to continue expanding and contracting for hundreds of years to maintain a constant population.

Short of some catastrophic change in death rate or fertility rate, the United States will experience population growth for 70 years beyond the point at which we drop our present fertility rate of 2.4 to 2.11 children per family. In effect, we will be sitting on a

---

[12] For more details on U. S. population growth see the two reports published by the Population Reference Bureau, "The Future Population of the U.S.," February, 1971, and "Toward a U.S. Population Policy," June, 1971; and O. Callahan, ed., *The American Population* Debate. New York: Doubleday, 1971.

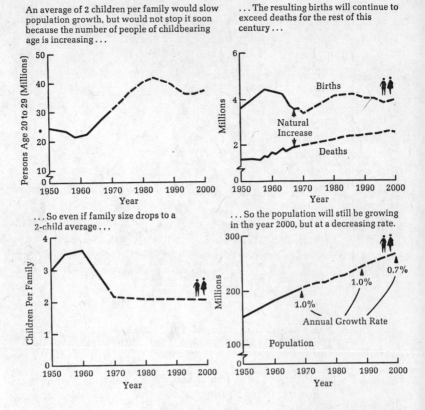

An average of 2 children per family would slow population growth, but would not stop it soon because the number of people of childbearing age is increasing...

... The resulting births will continue to exceed deaths for the rest of this century...

... So even if family size drops to a 2-child average...

... So the population will still be growing in the year 2000, but at a decreasing rate.

Figure 2–6 Why even the two-child family won't stop U.S. population growth by the year 2000. (Source: Interim report of the Commission on Population Growth and the American Future, March, 1971.)

population time bomb through about 1985, when the increase in potential mothers has peaked out. Some demographers [13] are concerned that the present slight decline in fertility rate might be reversed. Conceivably the present decrease could merely represent a delay in having children because of the economic recession, or couples may return again to the three-child family because of ir-

---

[13] Testimony by Philip M. Hauser, University of Chicago, before Special Sub-Committee on Human Resources, United States Senate, Committee on Labor and Public Welfare, Washington, D.C., October 14, 1971.

responsible and misleading reports in the press that the U.S. population problem has been solved.

Thus, immediate zero population growth is probably not desirable or even possible. Too rapid a population change could cause serious economic and social problems. However, it seems urgent that the attainment of zero population growth in the next 30 to 40 years with a population of around 270-million Americans should be one of our nation's primary goals. Such a goal will probably require a reduction of fertility to around 1.8 children per family or to around 2 children per family if immigration is sharply curtailed. This calls for continued increase in making birth-control information and devices readily available to anyone who wants them. But this will still not solve our problem. At present, most couples want too many children relative to our environmental predicament, and family planning alone, although a very important and useful service, merely helps a couple space the desired number of children over the fertile years. It is estimated [14] that less than 3 percent of childbearing women in the world practice birth control even though a far greater percentage have knowledge of and access to birth-control methods.

What would it be like to live in a society with zero population growth? Would there be economic stagnation? Economist Stephen Enke [15] of General Electric's TEMPO research group has worked out some models that indicate that slower or stable population growth may be an economic boon. Total GNP would be less but per capita GNP would be much higher, as shown below.

	GNP	Per Capita Income	Population
Present Fertility Rate	2.8 trillion	$ 9,219	308 million
Zero Population Growth	2.6 trillion	$10,404	256 million

Some industries, for example, those based on children, would decline, others would remain stationary, and some would grow.

---

[14] R. A. Falk, *This Endangered Planet*. New York: Random House, 1971, p. 157.

[15] Stephen Enke, *Zero U.S. Population Growth — When, How, and Why*, General Electric Co., TEMPO Center for Advanced Studies, 1970.

Nevertheless, society would be different. The age structure would change drastically with the median age rising from its current 27 to about 37, and the number of people older than 65 would about equal those under 15, as shown in Table 2-5.

Table 2–5   Age distribution in U.S. population.*

Age	1970	2020 (if fertility rate remains same as at present)	2020 (if fertility rate approaches zero growth)	2037 (ultimate stationary population at zero growth)
0-14	28.3%	25.3%	21.0%	20.3%
15-64	61.9	64.8	66.0	63.7
65 and over	9.8	10.0	13.0	16.0
Median age	27.9	32.4	35.7	37.3

*Source: U.S. Census Bureau

With an older age structure there may be fewer opportunities for advancement. Also, some observers fear that an older population might lose its spark and innovative spirit, although this is not borne out by the population of Sweden. With fewer children the financial dependency load on families would be lowered. This could be used to reduce expenditures for education or permit an increase in spending per pupil. In any event if the present younger generation decides to move towards zero population growth, it can have it both ways by insuring that as oldsters they by their numbers maintain control over society.

In summary, we should be wary of any projections concerning future population growth unless the author has considered the three major factors in population dynamics. Knowing the unpredictability of human beings, even then we should be cautious.

1. *Birth rate* minus *death rate*

2. *Age structure:* Particularly the number of women from ages 0 to 29.

3. *Total fertility rate:* The average number of children per woman between ages 15 and 45.

2–4 Population Density — The Population Implosion

Another population characteristic is that of population density, or distribution, that is, the number of people per square mile or other unit of area. Although this is not a factor directly affecting population growth, it is a key factor in determining the quality of life.

In addition to the population explosion we have a "population implosion." More and more of the world's peoples are migrating to urban centers. To an increasing number, many of these implosion centers could be more accurately described as "megaloptic monstrosities." This systematic urbanization of the planet will almost certainly continue as mechanization of agriculture and industrialization displace more and more people from rural areas to cities where many but not enough jobs are available.

Two out of three Americans now live in urban areas and nine out of ten of us will probably be living in such areas by 2000. After all, you can't expect to add the population equivalent of a city of about 250,000 persons every month without stopping for the next 30 years and expect very many of us to be living in the countryside. The United States Bureau of Census projects an addition of 75 to 100 million Americans between 1970 and 2000. Assuming an addition of 87 million Americans means an addition of 242,000 persons for each of the 360 months between 1970 and

---

[16] A more sophisticated study of population involves an analysis of several other factors, such as the mother's age at the birth of her first child. The reader interested in more details on population change might consult W. Petersen, *Population,* The Macmillan Co., 1969 and W. S. Thompson and D. T. Lewis, *Population Problems,* 5th ed., McGraw-Hill Book Co., 1965.

2000. During the 1960's our farm population dropped from 15 to 10 million. More than 75 percent of our population growth during this period occurred in metropolitan areas, with the suburbs absorbing most of it. Suburbanites now outnumber those living in central cities.[17] U.S. urban areas are now doubling in population at about the same rate as India, that is every 27 years.

In underdeveloped nations the majority of the population is still rural, but rapid urbanization is occurring, with 40 percent of their population expected to be urban dwellers by 2000.[18] Because of the economic plight of such countries, urbanization represents an even greater socially disrupting force. Take Turkey as an example, where at present about 27-million people live in rural areas and 7 million live in its cities. Its population is doubling every 27 years, and by 2010 it is estimated that Turkey will have 20 million in rural areas and 90 million in its cities — a growth in city population from 7 to 90 milllion in only about 40 years.[19] Where will a country in the early stages of industrialization find the jobs, houses, schools, and other services for these urban dwellers?

Some[20] have argued that the only real population problem in the United States is that of unbalanced population distribution. They say that too many of us live in urban centers. The Commission on Population Growth and the American Future has recognized that this is an overly simplistic interpretation of our problem. Obviously, population distribution is a factor, but formulating policies to encourage more citizens to move to rural areas (where jobs are scarce) does not eliminate the necessity for deciding whether or not we want to carry out such a policy for 300-, 400-, or 500-million Americans.[21]

---

[17] U.S. Bureau of Census, *Statistical Abstract of the U.S. — 1971*, U.S. Government Printing Office, Washington, D.C.

[18] Davis, Kingsley, "The Urbanization of the Human Population," *Scientific American*, 213, 40 (1965).

[19] Anderson, L., "People, Food and Cities in the Years Ahead," paper given at AID symposium on agriculture, Ankara, Turkey, March, 1969.

[20] National Goals Research Staff, *Toward Balanced Growth: Quantity with Quality*, Report to the President, U.S. Government Printing Office, Washington, D.C., 1970, Chapter 2.

[21] For more details on urban growth in the United States see the October, 1970 issue of *The Futurist*, World Future Society, Washington, D.C.

What will happen? The population story is told with two very simple curves. In a closed spaceship system with finite resources, the growth of population and the use of resources and energy will not continue indefinitely, and the "J" curve *will* be leveled off to an "S" curve when the system is brought into equilibrium, as shown in Figure 2-7. In other words, the system will eventually be

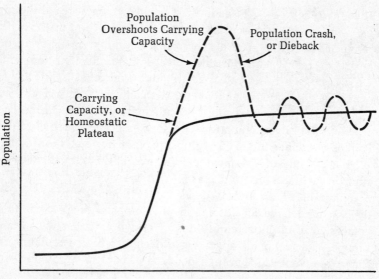

Figure 2-7   The conversion of the J-curve to an S-curve when a population overshoots the carrying capacity of its environment. A significant portion of the population is eliminated in a massive dieback and the population typically fluctuates around the carrying-capacity value.

brought into a steady state where birth rate equals death rate and we have zero population change. (The term zero population growth, or ZPG, is sometimes used. Strictly speaking, it represents the attainment of equilibrium in a period of growth, as we are experiencing now.)

or

Zero Population Change (ZPC)

Birth rate (BR) — Death rate (DR) $= 0$

or

Birth rate (BR) $=$ Death rate (DR)

These two curves — "J" and "S" — yield two radically different fates. The S-curve represents a population living in harmony with its environment; the J-curve represents a population ignoring or unaware of reality and hurtling toward instability, famine, and sharply increased death rates. The equilibrium level is known as the carrying capacity, or homeostatic plateau, and it represents the population that can be supported adequately by the resources available. When overpopulation of a species occurs relative to the resources available for maintaining life, then a population crash, or dieback — one of the most chilling words in our language — occurs through starvation, disease, or in the case of man warfare and man-induced ecological catastrophe. Some animals (apparently not man) have an automatic physiological mechanism that decreases fertility under conditions of crowding and stress. Man, of course, as a "rational" species can decide to limit population in order to prevent undesirable death-rate control through war, famine, disease, and eco-catastrophe.

So far man has had an advantage over many species. Through technological changes and revolutions he has been able to raise the carrying capacity, or homeostatic plateau. Some examples of technological innovations that provide increased carrying capacity are the bow and arrow, the domestication of animals, the cultivation of plants, the industrial revolution, and atomic energy. With each innovation the human population has risen sharply, as shown in Figure 2-8.[22] We appear to be in a very critical transi-

---

[22] The astute student of mathematics will realize that the terms J-curve and S-curve, while extremely useful, are somewhat imprecise mathematically. By expanding or contracting, or excessively distorting the scale of a plot, it is possible to make almost any curve a J-curve,

tion period moving rapidly on a J-curve toward a new homeostatic plateau (S-curve) with respect to resources and the disruption of our environment through too many people using too much energy.

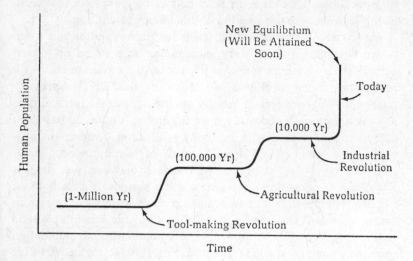

Figure 2–8   Man's ability to extend carrying capacity through technological innovation. The periodic transition from a J-curve to an S-curve. (Source: E. S. Deevy, Jr., "The Human Population," *Scientific American*, September, 1960 p. 52.)

The first major increase in population occurred after man learned to hunt more efficiently and to make his life more secure by learning how to make tools and more effective weapons. A hundred-thousand years later the carrying capacity was raised again when man began to change from a migrating hunter to a farmer with a more or less fixed abode. In this period of agricultural revolution the main sources of power were wind, water, and muscle.

After about 10,000 years a third major increase in population began. It occurred around 1750 as a result of the industrial revolu-

---

S-curve, or a straight line. The scales in the J-curves and S-curves used in this text were selected to present the situation realistically. In Figure 2–8, in order to show major changes in population over a greater range of time, a log-log scale was used. This allows both variables to increase regularly by factors of ten.

tion. It was really an energy revolution based on supplementing and replacing much muscular energy with machines running on the chemical energy stored in our finite supply of fossil fuels. Towns and cities formed and grew rapidly as people clustered around their machines. Of course, at least half of the people in the world have yet to share in the benefits of this energy revolution.

We are now discovering that the industrial revolution has a bill which is coming due. Its very success has been based on almost completely ignoring its massive impact on the environment. As a result, the coming revolution, or transition, must involve preserving our life-support system, not by raising our population and consumption, but by deliberately lowering them. It must be based on using knowledge to live in harmony with nature, rather than attempting to dominate and simplify nature to meet our needs.

There are several important differences between our present situation and those in the past transition periods from a J- to an S-curve. For the first time man has no place to migrate in significant numbers. We are using essentially all of the inhabitable land on our ship. We shall see later that as a solution to our population problem going into space is one of our most naive myths. Also for the first time, there are so many of us and our energy and resource-using activities are so great that we can potentially disrupt or even destroy the life-support system for the entire ship. Because of this and the second law of thermodynamics, we shall see that there is ultimately no completely technological solution to the population-pollution problem.

We should also recognize that there are two types of homeostatic plateaus with respect to the human population, as shown in Figure 2-9. One level is the maximum or upper limit, that is, the carrying capacity. Living at this limit means survival for most passengers, but at a terrible cost. Essentially, all passengers would be living lives of degradation, regimentation, and misery, just above starvation levels. This is the state in which at least half of our passengers exist today. It would probably be achieved only after a massive dieback of billions when population momentum carried us past the maximum level. The other level is that of an optimum not a maximum population, a level that would allow all passengers to have a quality life and their fair share of the planet's resources.

At present no one knows precisely what these optimum and maximum levels are. Many observers feel, however, that we

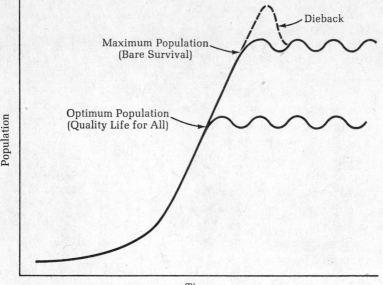

Figure 2–9   Two levels of population. One involves bare survival
for all and the other involves the opportunity for a quality life for all.

have already exceeded the optimum population level and that the
maximum population will be reached within the next 30 to 50
years,[23] unless man begins now to control his cancerous growth
in numbers and use of energy and resources.

The only real question is not whether the J-curve will be leveled to an S-curve, but when and how much pain and misery we
will have to endure in the process. We are beginning to realize
that lowering the death rate by providing food and health care
without *simultaneously* decreasing the birth rate sharply is an in-

[23] See National Academy of Sciences, *Resources and Man*, W. H.
Freeman, 1969, p. 5; H. R. Hulett, "Optimum World Population,"
Bioscience 20, 160 (1970); O. R. Allen, "Population, Resources and the
Great Complexity," Population Reference Bureau Selection No. 29,
Population Reference Bureau, Washington, D.C., 1969, p. 4, and S. F.
Singer, ed., *Is There an Optimum Level of Population?* New York:
McGraw-Hill, 1971. See also section 7-4 of this book.

humane practice that sentences an even greater number to death at a later date.

There are only two solutions. One is a rational decision to lower the birth rate on the ship sharply, not slowly as we are doing now. It means giving up our assumed freedoms to have as many children as we want and to use vast amounts of the ship's resources in a wasteful manner in order to have breathable air and drinkable water and in order to have a free and peaceful world with quality lives for all of the passengers.

The other is a monstrously inhumane solution that involves continuing on our present course, a course that must eventually condemn to death not millions but billions of passengers as the death-rate curve rises. While you ate dinner today some 1,400 [24] human beings on this spaceship died of starvation, malnutrition, or diseases resulting from these weakened conditions. By this time tomorrow 34,000 will have starved, 238,000 by next week and approximately 15,000,000 by next year. If it makes you feel better, use the lower estimate of 5-million starvation deaths per year and divide all these numbers by three. This doesn't really change the stark reality of the problem. Half are children under five. Many talk about famines in the 1970's, 1980's, or 1990's. By comparing the present starvation and malnutrition death rate of 5 to 20 million each year with previous major famines involving 3 to 10 million (see Table 1-2), it is apparent that the world's greatest famine is occurring right now. To avoid facing reality we conveniently classify starvation as a famine only if it occurs in a particular country rather than on a global basis.

This death rate each year is over 21 times that of all Americans killed in all our wars. Even so, these casualties are replaced by present population growth in only 2½ months. One can begin to see that if we allow nature to control our exploding population by the death-rate solution, then we are sentencing billions to death. Remember that a billion people represents about five times the

---

[24] R. Dumont, *The Hungry Future*. New York: Frederick A. Praeger, 1969, p. 35 and P. R. Ehrlich and A. H. Ehrlich, *Population Resources and Environment*, W. H. Freeman, 1970. These sources estimate that 10 to 20 million starve each year. Other estimates put the lowest figure around 5 million. Even with these lower figures, about 500 persons starved to death while you had dinner.

present U.S. population. The spread of disease from the health implications of such a catastrophe could easily eliminate one to several billion additional human beings. Thinking about these unthinkable things may help us act to prevent such a nightmarish future for our children and grandchildren by drastically lowering our birth and consumption rates over the next 30 to 50 years. The choice is ours.

In our plastic, technological cocoon many of us have become insulated from nature,[25] ignorant of the meaning of large numbers and growth rates, and desensitized to the agonies and needs of our fellow passengers.

Add to the J-curve of increasing agony in the underdeveloped countries the fact that we in the developed countries are threatening the entire life-support system by rounding the bend on two other J-curves, that is, increasing use of energy and finite resources and the resulting pollution. During four days in April, 1970, millions of people watched and prayed as the lives of three astronauts were saved on Apollo 13, a spaceship in trouble. During those same four days back on spaceship earth, some 116,000 human beings died of starvation or malnutrition. These were unique human beings, not numbers and not things.

This summarizes our problem. We are finally beginning to realize the nature and complexity of this human dilemma. This awareness is our hope and challenge. But to act wisely we must become ecologically informed.

Not to decide is to decide.

Harvey Cox

---

[25] For example, many affluent Americans going from one heated or airconditioned environment to another have the illusion that airconditioning and heating systems remove air pollutants.

3

Two Spaceship Laws We Can't Repeal

3–1 Scientific Laws

We have discussed the passengers on our ship. Let us now examine some of the fundamental scientific laws determining what the passengers can and cannot do. If you pick up an apple and then let it go, you would automatically expect it to drop to the floor or other surface below it. Why? Because during your lifetime and apparently during the lifetime of all others on this spaceship, unsupported objects have always been observed to fall downward. This description of what we have always observed has been codified in what we call the Law of Gravity. This and other scientific laws are descriptions of the orderly behavior of nature based solely on observation of what always happens on our spaceship. (In space or on another planet a different set of laws may, of course, apply.) Unlike legal laws passed by man, we can't repeal these natural limitations on what we can or cannot do. A scientific theory, on the other hand, may be altered or even overthrown. It is an attempt to explain the law. You may doubt Einstein's theory explaining gravitation, but I am confident you would not jump off of a ten-story building with the idea that you would not fall or that you would slowly float to the ground.

Yet, in a way this is precisely what we seem to be trying to do. We are not trying to ignore the Law of Gravity, but we are acting as if we could ignore or repeal two equally fundamental and inviolable laws on our spaceship, the <u>First and Second Laws of Thermodynamics</u>.

What happens in terms of energy when an apple drops to the floor? Potential energy is the energy associated with the position of an object relative to some force that can act upon it. When the apple is dropped we say that there is a loss of potential energy from a high value (hand) to a low value (floor). It has dropped to a state of minimum potential energy relative to its surroundings. (Under other circumstances, it may drop to a lower value of potential energy. For example, suppose the floor was on the fifth story of a building.)

Does this mean that we have lost or consumed energy in this process? It is important to distinguish between the <u>system</u> (that is, the collection of matter under study) and its <u>environment</u>, or <u>surroundings</u> (i.e., the rest of the universe). During any process energy may pass from the system to the surroundings or from the surroundings to the system.

According to the *First Law of Thermodynamics,* which is the familiar *Law of Conservation of Energy,* energy is neither created nor destroyed in any process. It is merely transformed from one form to another, such as heat, light, mechanical, electrical, or chemical energy. If the system loses or gains energy, then an equal amount of energy must be transferred in some form to or from the surroundings. In any process, the total energy of the system plus its surroundings remains constant.

First Law of Thermodynamics —
Law of Conservation of Energy

In all chemical and physical changes, energy is neither created nor destroyed but merely transformed from one form to another.[1]

or

In any process the total energy of the system plus its surroundings remains constant.

---

[1] Matter can be converted into energy (witness nuclear power) but this becomes measurable only in nuclear reactions, not ordinary chemical reactions. A more accurate and comprehensive statement would be that "matter-energy can be neither created nor destroyed."

In terms of the apple, potential energy is transformed primarily into the average energy of motion (kinetic energy) of the apple and into the average energy of motion (kinetic energy) of the air molecules in the surroundings. Temperature[2] is a measure of the average energy of motion of a collection of molecules. The net effect is to raise the temperature of the air molecules of the immediate surroundings and we say that heat has been transferred from the system to the surroundings, as shown in Figure 3–1.

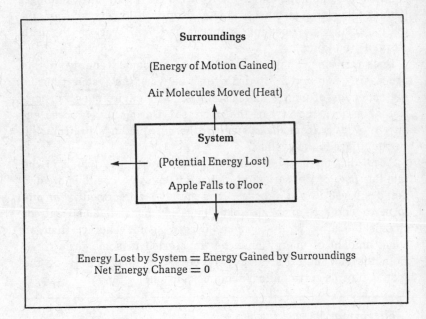

Figure 3–1   Illustration of the Law of Conservation of Energy — the First Law of Thermodynamics.

Most of us are familiar with and have accepted the First Law of Thermodynamics. Why belabor the obvious? The answer to this question lies in the fact that we tend to forget that we can't get

---

[2] Actually we should speak only of the absolute, or Kelvin, temperature as an average kinetic energy of a collection of molecules. The Kelvin temperature is obtained by adding 273 to the temperature in degrees centigrade.

something for nothing. For example, in terms of feeding our growing list of passengers, many talk of making synthetic foods as a solution to our problem. To make synthetic foods requires that we use an energy source, normally fossil fuels or perhaps nuclear energy, to force small molecules together to form the large organic molecules that comprise food. As a result of the first law, this will require that we put in at least as much energy as we eventually get out of the molecules in terms of food energy. This assumes that our process is 100 percent efficient. Actually even our most sophisticated processes approach only 60 percent efficiency. In other words, to make synthetic foods on a large scale would require more energy than we would get out of it. We would have to deplete even more rapidly our dwindling supply of high-energy resources in the form of fossil fuels and uranium, and add enormous amounts of heat and other pollutants to our environment. And this does not even take into account the additional heat and chemical pollution added by building the food plants, extracting and transporting raw materials to the plants, and the transportation and distribution systems needed to get the synthetic food to the users. There is no such thing as a free lunch on our spaceship.

3–3   If You Think Things Are Mixed Up Now, Just Wait — The Second Law of Thermodynamics

Sir C. P. Snow, distinguished literary figure and scientist, made a statement to the effect that not being able to describe the Second Law of Thermodynamics is equivalent to admitting that you have never read a work of Shakespeare. While the first law is concerned with the total distribution of energy in various forms in any process, the second law is based on describing the direction of flow of energy in processes.

In nature we can distinguish between two types of processes, spontaneous processes which can occur naturally without an outside input of energy and nonspontaneous processes which do require an energy input from the surroundings. The second law is a summary of our observations of the direction of flow of energy in spontaneous processes.

What are some spontaneous processes? We observe that objects fall to the ground, water flows spontaneously downhill, and heat flows spontaneously from a hot body to a cold body. Closer observation reveals that all spontaneous processes have one common element based on the phenomena of order and disorder. In general, do you observe that things and events tend spontaneously to become more orderly or more disorderly? What is the most probable state of your room — naturally increasing order or naturally increasing chaos? To keep it neat and orderly doesn't your room require a continuous input of outside energy on your part?

Houses do not spontaneously acquire new coats of paint. They tend spontaneously to fall into disrepair. If you shuffle an ordered deck of cards arranged by suits, you get a disordered deck. But if you shuffle a disordered deck, you do not expect it spontaneously to become arranged by suits. The probability of such an event is vanishingly small, because there is only one perfectly orderly state for the deck, but there are millions of possible disordered arrangements for the 52 cards. If you drop a vase to the floor and it shatters, you would under no circumstances expect the random array of fragments to return spontaneously to re-form the vase. We cannot put Humpty Dumpty together again, at least not spontaneously.

The natural state of vegetation on the land is a higgledy-piggledy disorderly state, at least as viewed from above in an airplane. Lawns must be cut to keep them orderly. A garden or field, consisting of neat and orderly rows of plants, does not form spontaneously. Fly over the land and you can immediately see where man has been by the presence of straight lines in such things as fields, roads, and houses. These lines represent an ordering process against the apparently natural tendency for the more random, or disorderly, growth of vegetation. These ordering activities of man are nonspontaneous processes requiring enormous and continuous inputs of energy for their maintenance.

If a highly ordered crystal of food coloring is added to a glass of water, the dye molecules spontaneously spread throughout the solution and their relative disorder increases. If a woman wearing

---

[3] The relative degree of order or disorder is dependent on the level of observation. For example, at the molecular level we would view vegetation as a highly ordered array of molecules.

perfume walks into the room, in a few minutes the molecules of the scent will diffuse rapidly throughout the room.

Smoke from a smokestack and exhaust from an automobile spread out spontaneously to become more randomly dispersed in the atmosphere. The dumping of chemical or other wastes into a river or other body of water is based on the assumption that they will be spontaneously dispersed and diluted into a more disordered or randomized state.

Indeed our overall approach to pollution control to date has been based on the concept that "dilution is the solution to pollution." We dump our wastes into the air, water, or soil and assume that they will spontaneously be diluted to harmless amounts or at least dispersed far away from us. As we shall see later, we are now beginning to realize that *dilution is not the solution to pollution*. It is a useful application of the idea that disorder tends naturally to increase. However, it contains some fatal flaws.

We have apparently uncovered a driving force for spontaneity — the tendency toward increasing disorder.

A Tentative Hypothesis — The Increasing Disorder Principle

A *system* tends spontaneously toward increasing disorder, or randomness.

But do we always observe this in nature? Can we find examples of spontaneous processes that do not involve an increase in disorder in the system? Is a living organism, such as man, an example of increasing disorder? Instead, the formation and maintenance of a living organism give a vivid demonstration of the transformation of disorder into order in the system. An array of atoms and molecules is synthesized to form a highly organized living cell. These cells then multiply and arrange themselves into even more highly organized forms. This process appears to contradict the tendency towards disorder. But the maintaining of life is not a spontaneous process. To form and preserve the highly ordered arrangement of molecules and organized network of chemical reactions in your body, you must supply it with energy and raw materials from the environment. In other words, order in the body system is maintained at the expense of a greater increase in disorder in the environment. The production of food, the manufacturing of various chemicals, clothes, shelter, and other supplies, the burning of fossil fuels to provide heat and to cook foods all result in increases in disorder of the environment, particularly in the form of heat or the disorderly, chaotic motion of molecules.

The spontaneous tendency is for your body to decay. Its large molecules, organized in one place, have a natural tendency to be broken down into smaller molecules, particularly carbon dioxide and water, and dispersed throughout the atmosphere. This natural tendency for increasing disorder, which finally results in death, is held in check only by continued inputs of energy and matter that result in increased disorder in the environment. Man struggles during his lifetime to maintain a small island of order in an ocean of increasing disorder. Minutes after death the universe is more disordered than it was before we were born. Man can create temporary domains of order, but attempting to create order on a universal scale is like trying to freeze the Atlantic Ocean with a small ice cube.

Photosynthesis also seems to contradict the increasing disorder hypothesis, because it results in the conversion of small molecules (carbon dioxide and water) into large and highly organized molecules in a living plant. But here we run into the larger increases in disorder in our solar system. Photosynthesis depends on solar energy. Nuclear fusion reactions in the sun produce astronomical amounts of disorder as heat and other forms of energy — a massive increase in disorder and heat that swamps the relatively tiny increase in order represented by life on earth.

Thus, when we consider the change in disorder in both the system and surroundings we always find a net increase in disorder for any spontaneous process. Experimental measurements again and again have revealed that for any spontaneous process, when one looks at both the system and its surroundings, there is always a net increase in disorder. We need these facts to revise our original hypothesis to include both the system plus its environment, or surroundings.

Revised Hypothesis — The Increasing Disorder Principle

Any system plus its surroundings tends spontaneously toward increasing disorder, or randomness.

This is a statement of the *Second Law of Thermodynamics*. Scientists frequently use the term entropy as being a measure of relative disorder. We use the terms entropy and disorder of a system or its surroundings interchangeably.

Entropy

Entropy   = Measure of relative disorder

High entropy = Disorder

Low entropy = Order

We can now restate the Second Law of Thermodynamics in terms of disorder, or entropy.

The Second Law of Thermodynamics

(The Increasing Disorder, or Entropy, Principle)

Any system plus its surroundings tends spontaneously towards a state of increasing entropy, or disorder

or

Any spontaneous process results in a net increase in disorder, or entropy, when both the system and its environment, or surroundings, are considered.

It should be emphasized that the second law makes no predictions about the system only. It must include an analysis of the entropy changes in both the system and its surroundings. Most "apparent" violations of the second law involve situations in which the observer fails to include the greater entropy increase in the surroundings where there is an increase in order in the system. The net result is still a spontaneous increase in total entropy.

In a closed system, such as our spaceship, the second law determines the ultimate limit of what we can and cannot do. It tells us that maintaining order in the form of life *always* results in an increase in disorder in our surroundings. It also tells us that as we try to support more and more humans at higher and higher levels of energy and resource consumption, the result will automatically be increasing disorder in our life-support system.

According to the first law, the total energy of the universe remains constant. However, the second law states that as energy is transformed from one form of energy to another it is degraded into less and less useful forms and eventually ends up primarily as heat or molecular disorder. A useful form of energy is one that has a high capacity for doing work. For example, the change in potential energy of the apple enabled it to perform work as it dropped by moving the air molecules. We could have tied a string to the apple and used a pulley to have the apple perform work as it fell by lifting some object lighter than the apple. Energy in the form of heat in the environment is practically useless. It is in the form of the chaotic, disorganized motion of molecules and cannot be harnessed readily to perform work. The end result is that essentially all of the ordering processes necessary for life on our spaceship result in an increase in disorder, primarily in the form of heat in our life-support system, as shown in Figure 3–2. *The ultimate pollutant in any spaceship is heat.*

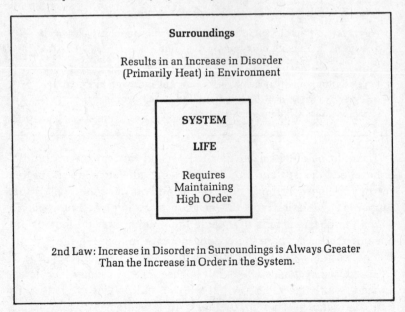

Surroundings

Results in an Increase in Disorder
(Primarily Heat) in Environment

SYSTEM

LIFE

Requires
Maintaining
High Order

2nd Law: Increase in Disorder in Surroundings is Always Greater
Than the Increase in Order in the System.

Figure 3–2   The Second Law of Thermodynamics. Not only can we not get something for nothing but we always lose in the process.

We can summarize the first and second laws as follows:

The second law means that whenever we attempt to order a part
of nature the disorder created in our environment exceeds the
order created in the system. As Robert Morse put it, "the second
law means that it is easier and cheaper to get into trouble than to
get out of it."[4]

3—4   Our Arrogant Use of the Term "Spaceship Earth"

In real life there are two major types of systems, open and
closed. An open system is one in which both matter and energy
are exchanged between a system and its surroundings. A closed
system is one in which energy but not matter is exchanged between the system and its surroundings.

[4] Address to the National Research Council, Washington D.C.,
March 21, 1971.

An open container of boiling water is an example of an open system. Both energy and matter are being exchanged between the container of water and the surrounding atmosphere. All living organisms are also examples of open systems. We take energy and matter into our bodies, transform them to maintain life, and put heat and waste materials back into our surroundings. Thus, life is an open, or flowing, system, maintained only by a balanced exchange of matter and energy with the environment. This balanced input and output maintains the steady state needed for survival. We can therefore describe life in an individual organism in terms of matter and energy as *an open system maintained in a steady state.*

We have seen earlier that this does not violate the Second Law of Thermodynamics. Our highly ordered steady-state system is maintained only at the expense of increased disorder in our environment. When we add up the total order and disorder in a steady-state system plus its surroundings, there is always a net increase in disorder, or entropy, usually in the form of heat added to the environment.

Let us examine some closed systems. Consider a closed test tube containing chemicals. It can be heated or cooled and thus gain or lose energy, but the amount of matter in the system remains the same even though the chemicals can react to form different substances.

A man living in a space capsule is another example of a closed system. Once the capsule is closed, he can only stay alive as long as there is an energy input from outside (solar energy to recharge the batteries for his power system) and a system capable of recycling the chemicals needed to maintain life. Our man-made space capsules cannot sustain life very long; they must be brought back to earth periodically, converted to an open system, and refilled with supplies.

In this sense they are not really spaceships but crude and inefficient imitations of a truly self-sustaining closed system. In this sense the only real spaceship, or closed system, we have is the earth. We can never return or go anywhere to take on new supplies. (Even though a handful of astronauts have left earth, they have had to carry a temporary life-support system with them, and must return to the mother ship in order to survive.) Life on this closed system depends on a delicate and intricate array of chemical recycling systems developed through millions of years of evolution and driven and sustained by energy from the sun.

One of the purposes of this book is to show the bankruptcy of the term "spaceship earth" as it is normally used by man. This term has meaning to most of us because we liken the earth to our man-made spacecrafts. This is an upside-down view of reality and is yet another manifestation of our arrogance towards nature. The question is not how the earth is like a spaceship but how a spaceship is like the earth. The only real spaceship is the earth and man-made crafts are, relatively speaking, crude toys designed by people living on a large spaceship.

We should delight in the fact that we did not plan and build spaceship earth. On our man-made spaceships every natural function can be performed only after the utmost deliberation and rigid control. There is little room for novelty, spontaneity, freedom, or most of the things that make life rich, vivid, or poignant. In order to survive on a man-made spaceship, everything must be programmed. Our life would be managed and manipulated by experts, swathed in artificiality, and surrounded by gadgetry. How would you like to spend your entire lifetime on such a voyage?

Because we have the spaceship image backwards, we have not cared about the real ship. There has seemed to be enough fuel to keep us going, and as for later generations, that is their problem. Our task is not to learn how to pilot spaceship earth. It is not to learn how — as Teilhard de Chardin would have it — "to seize the tiller of the world." Our task is to give up our fantasies of omnipotence. In other words, we must stop trying to steer. The solution to our present dilemma does not lie in attempting to extend our technical and managerial skills into every sphere of existence. *Thus, from a human standpoint our environmental crisis is the result of our arrogance towards nature.*

Somehow we must tune our senses again to the beat of existence, sensing in nature fundamental rhythms we can trust even though we may never fully understand them. We must learn anew that it is we who belong to the earth and not the earth to us. This rediscovery of our finitude is fundamental to any genuinely human future.

3–5. The Environmental Crisis is an Entropy Crisis

We have discussed the fact that man's energy-use processes are very inefficient with most of the energy being lost as heat to the environment. One way to improve the situation would be to increase the efficiency of some of our energy-conversion processes. For example, the internal-combustion engine has an efficiency of about 10 to 12 percent. When we deduct other friction losses the automobile is only about 5 percent efficient; 95 percent of the energy used to drive it is wasted and lost as heat to the environment.[5] If we sat down and tried to design the most thermodynamically inefficient engine possible, we would be hard pressed to come up with a poorer one than the internal-combustion engine.

Converting to steam engines would probably increase engine efficiency perhaps 30 to 40 percent, not to mention elimination of most of the harmful chemical pollutants spewing out of the exhausts of our automobiles. Improvement in efficiency would then be a major aid. Even so, the second law eventually imposes an upper limit on efficiency improvement. Although you can improve efficiency, the second law tells us that we can never reach 100 percent efficiency.

As we shall see throughout the remainder of this book, the second law provides the key for both understanding our environmental crisis, and for understanding how we must deal with this crisis. We have just seen that from a human standpoint the environmental crisis results from our arrogant view that nature is here to serve us, the masters. From a physical standpoint, however, the environmental crisis is an entropy, or disorder, crisis, resulting from our vain attempts to ignore the laws of thermodynamics. The second law explains why our arrogant view of nature won't work. According to the second law, any increase in order in the system will automatically and irrevocably require an even greater increase in entropy, or disorder, in the environment. Thus, paradoxically, as we increasingly attempt to order, or "con-

---

[5] For a summary of energy conversion efficiencies for various types of engines see John McHale, *The Ecological Context.* George Braziller, Inc., New York, 1970, p. 130-131.

quer," the earth we must inevitably put greater and greater stress on the environment. Failure to accept the fact that we can't repeal the First and Second Laws of Thermodynamics and that we must learn to live with the restrictions they impose on us can only lead to a steady degradation of the quality of life on this planet.

Why do we think we can ignore or repeal these laws? Part of our problem is one of ignorance. Most people have never heard of these laws or, if they have, they do not understand their implications. A more important factor is that these laws are statistical rather than individual. Everyone accepts the fact that he cannot violate the Law of Gravity because it limits him and everyone else on a personal level.

We have the illusion, however, that we can ignore the consequences of the second law. Each individual's activities increase the disorder in the environment, but individual impact has no major consequence. It is only when we have a large number of individuals living in a high-energy society that the statistical impact of all of their individual disorder-producing activities can affect the overall life-support system. The limitation and the challenge of the Second Law of Thermodynamics means that we are all interconnected whether we like it or not.

The Environmental Crisis Is

1. A crisis in human values — our attempts to order nature.
2. An entropy crisis — our attempts to ignore the Second Law of Thermodynamics.

The imperative that we should learn from thermodynamics is simple and profound: *whenever you do anything be sure to take into account its present and possible future impact on your fellow passengers and your environment.* This is an ecological imperative that we must apply now if we are to prevent a drastic degradation of life for all passengers on our beautiful and fragile craft.

The law that entropy increases — the Second Law of Thermodynamics — holds, I think, the supreme position among laws of nature. If someone points out to you that your pet theory of the universe is in disagreement with Maxwell's equations — then so much the worse for Maxwell's equations. If it is found to be contradicted by observation — well, these experimentalists do bungle things sometimes. But if your theory is found to be against the Second Law of Thermodynamics, I can give you no hope; there is nothing to do but collapse in deepest humiliation.

Arthur S. Eddington,
Noted British astronomer, in the Gifford lectures of 1927

4

Our Life-Support System

4–1   Solar Energy and the Biosphere

What is our basic survival equipment? We must begin with the energy source that sustains all life on earth, that is, radiant energy from the sun. The life-supporting functions of this solar energy consist of warming the earth and of initiating the process of photosynthesis in plants, which provide nutrients to sustain all life. The sun consists mostly of hydrogen maintained in its interior at temperatures which may be as high as 10 million°C. Under such high temperatures and pressures four hydrogen nuclei can be "fused" together to form a helium nucleus. This process of *nuclear fusion*, which releases enormous quantities of energy is the ultimate source of energy for life on this planet. The sun is thus a gigantic thermonuclear, or hydrogen, bomb undergoing continuous explosion that liberates about 100,000,000,000,000,000,000,000,000 calories of energy every second. If we could completely harness this energy, each person on earth each second would have for his own personal use over 70,000 times the annual power consumption of the United States. The sun loses about 4.2-million tons of mass every second in order to produce this enormous amount of energy. Assuming an automobile weighs about two tons, or 4000 pounds, this means that every second the sun loses the mass equivalent to that found in over 2-million automobiles. We should not become alarmed, however, that the sun will run out of fuel. It has probably been in existence for at least 6-billion years, and there is enough hydrogen left to keep it going for at least 8-billion years more.

The sun radiates energy in all directions. In terms of the solar system, the earth represents a very small target, and only about one two-billionths of the sun's energy reaches the earth's outer atmosphere. Even this tiny fraction is equivalent in energy to about 100-million Hiroshima-size atomic bombs per day. This small amount reaching our atmosphere is a spectrum of radiant energy consisting of high-energy gamma rays, x-rays, and ultra-violet rays which can cause sunburn, and lower energy visible light and infra-red radiation.

More than half of this incoming radiation is reflected back into space or absorbed by atmospheric gases, clouds, and dust in our atmosphere. Most of the rest goes to heat the planet. Fortunately, our present atmosphere filters out almost all of the deadly high-energy gamma, x-ray, and ultra-violet radiation. Once through the atmosphere more energy is absorbed or reflected by the land and oceans.

As a result of these and other losses, a ridiculously small portion of the solar energy reaching us — probably no more than 2 percent — is actually used to support life through photosynthesis in plants. The only portion of the spectrum of solar energy that is finally used to support life is visible light. And even this form of energy can only be captured and used by plants containing chlorophyll or chlorophyll-like substances. Even so, plants use 100 times more energy than that used by all man-made machines and they make more efficient use of their share of the energy than any man-made machine. We have much to learn from plants in terms of the efficiency of energy conversion.

What makes up our life-support system into which this life-giving energy flows? All life is found in the biosphere, or ecosphere, a thin film of air, water, and soil having an approximate thickness of only nine miles. This life-support system consists of three major parts as summarized in Figure 4-1: (1) above us a thin layer of usable atmosphere no more than seven-miles high; (2) around us a supply of water in rivers, lakes, glaciers, oceans, and underground deposits, most of which is not available for drinking; and (3) below us a thin crust of soil, minerals, and rocks extending only a few thousand feet into the earth's interior, with only about 12 percent of this crust capable of being inhabited by man. Here we find our irreplaceable deposits of fossil fuels and ores which we are steadily depleting.

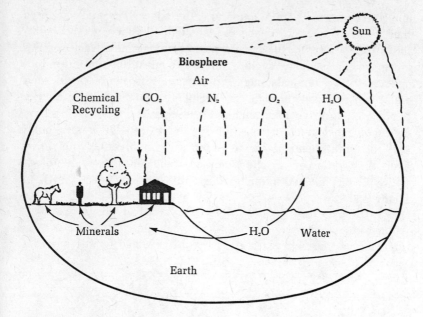

Figure 4–1 Major components of our life-support system, that is, the biosphere.

This remarkably intricate biofilm of life contains all of the water, minerals, oxygen, nitrogen, carbon dioxide, and other chemical building blocks that must be recycled again and again in order for life to continue. If we liken spaceship earth to an apple, then all life is found within the skin of the apple, a delicate skin that is being stressed by man at an alarming and rapidly increasing rate. Everything in this skin is interconnected and interdependent; the air helps purify the water, the water is used by plants and animals, and the plants help renew the air. It is a marvelous and mysterious system.

4–2 Life on Earth Depends on Energy Flow and Chemical Recycling

For all practical purposes the total amount of matter on our spaceship is fixed. In other words no matter enters or leaves the ship. (The amounts of matter represented by incoming meteors and other materials from space and the spaceships and satellites that we have put into space are negligible.) Since no new matter is lost or added, this means that chemicals necessary for life must be continuously cycled and recycled throughout the biosphere. Vital chemicals such as carbon, nitrogen, oxygen, and water are recycled through the biosphere, with the sun's energy being used to drive and sustain these chemical cycles — usually called *biogeochemical cycles* (*bio* for living, *geo* for water, rocks, and soil, and *chemical* for the processes involved). Note, however, that while certain chemicals are recycled, energy is not; it *flows* in only one direction through the biosphere, as shown in Figure 4-2.

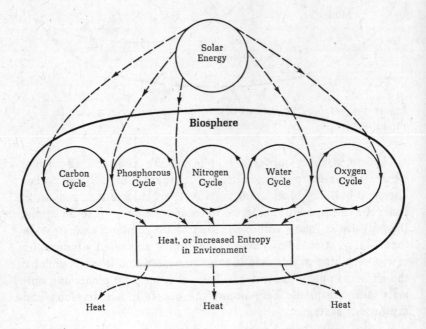

Figure 4–2   Life on spaceship earth depends on the cycling of critical chemicals and the one-way flow of energy through the biosphere. Dotted lines represent energy and solid lines represent chemicals.

Thus, all life on spaceship earth, or any truly closed system, depends on two important factors, namely, chemical recycling and energy flow.

1. Chemical recycling
2. One-way energy flow through the biosphere

4–3   What is an Ecosystem?

The biosphere can be viewed as being made up of a series of subsystems called ecological systems, or ecosystems. But in order to understand what an ecosystem is we must first look at all of the major components of the world around us.

What do we find in the universe? We find matter and energy undergoing various transformations, and a crude classification would divide the universe into three major domains: (1) the microscopic world of the very small (atoms, molecules, cells), (2) the macroscopic world of everyday objects, and (3) the supermacroscopic, or cosmic, world of the very large (planets, stars, and galaxies).

But matter in each of these domains is found to be organized in recognizable sublevels. A more detailed description of the structure of the world is obtained by looking at various levels of organization from a subatomic electron to a planet or galaxy, as summarized in Figure 4-3.

Ecology, the subject of this book, deals primarily with only three levels in this spectrum of matter — populations, communities, and ecosystems. Ecology, a term coined less than 100 years ago, is derived from two Greek words, oikos, meaning house or place to live and logos, meaning study of. Literally then, ecology is the study of organisms in their homes. It is usually defined as a study of the interrelationships of living organisms with each other and with their environment. Another way of looking at ecology is to consider it as a study of the structure and function of nature. In other words, what organisms and groups of organisms do we find in nature and what are they doing?

Let us begin with the structure of nature. A group of organisms of the same kind is called a population. Looking around in nature we find a number of populations of different organisms living

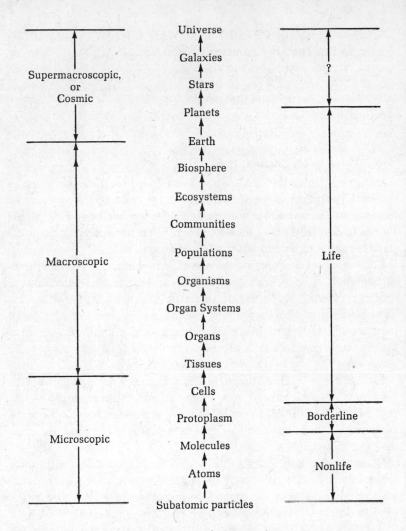

Figure 4–3 Levels of organization of matter.

together in a particular area. This grouping is called a community. If we add the nonliving environment of energy, air, water, soil, and other chemicals to all of the communities in a given area we have the next level of organization, that is, the ecosystem. If in turn we group together all of the various ecosystems on the planet we have the largest life unit of all, the biosphere.

Thus, an ecosystem can be as small as a fallen log or as large as the world. The major aquatic ecosystems are the familiar lakes, ponds, rivers, springs, swamps, estuaries, coral reefs, seas, and oceans. On land the major ecosystems — usually called biomes — are the forests, savannahs (combinations of grasslands with scattered trees or clumps of trees), chaparral (shrublands), grasslands, tundra, and deserts. A more detailed study of plant and animal ecology would reveal that each of these major types of ecosystems can be further divided. For example, in colder regions we have coniferous forests dominated by cold-resisting evergreen trees; in temperate regions deciduous, or leaf-shedding, forests of oaks, maples and beeches add to the beauty of our home, and in tropical areas we have the luxuriant rain forests.

The whole biosphere then can be visualized as a vast gradient of diverse ecosystems all interconnected in a complex three-dimensional fabric of life. Indeed the most important principle of ecology is that everything is connected to everything. Intruding into or disrupting an ecosystem in one place always has some complex, usually unpredictable, and frequently undesirable effect somewhere else. This backlash effect has been eloquently described by the English poet Francis Thompson:

"Thou canst not stir a flower without troubling a star."

The goal of ecology is to find out just how everything is connected in the biosphere. Ecology is a relatively young science and as a result we know relatively little at a time when man is running around in the biosphere much like a bull in a china shop.

Let's look at a particular ecosystem in more detail. What are the major components of any ecosystem and what major events are occurring in an ecosystem? An ecosystem can be divided into its nonliving and living components. The nonliving, or abiotic, portion consists of an outside <u>energy</u> source (usually solar energy) and the <u>chemicals</u> necessary for life. The living portion consists of <u>producers</u> (plants) and <u>consumers</u>. The consumers are usually divided into macroconsumers (the animals) and microconsumers, or decomposers (bacteria and fungi), as summarized below.

Nonliving Portion

Chemicals: The nonliving matter, water, oxygen, carbon dioxide, organic compounds, and other chemicals used by plants and animals. The critical nutrients are cycled through the biosphere in the biogeochemical cycles.

Energy: The solar energy that drives the entire system. It flows through the system, and at each level a small part of it is used to support life. Most of it is degraded to less useful forms and returned to the environment as heat or entropy in accordance with the Second Law of Thermodynamics.

Living Portion

Producers, or Plants: Ranging in size from tiny phytoplankton in water to giant trees, they provide food for themselves and other organisms by using solar energy to convert carbon dioxide and water to sugars and other important molecules by photosynthesis.

Macroconsumers, or Animals: Herbivores, such as deer, cows, rabbits, mice, grasshoppers, sheep, and zooplankton in water are the primary consumers that feed on plants. In turn, carnivorous animals, such as frogs, lizards, snakes, cats, wolves, and fish are secondary consumers that feed on herbivores. Finally, top carnivores, such as lions, hawks, and large fish can in turn feed on these animals. Omnivorous animals, such as man, are both herbivores and carnivores, feeding on both plants and other animals.

Microconsumers, or Decomposers: Tiny organisms, such as bacteria and fungi, that complete the cycle of chemicals by breaking down the dead animals and plants and returning their chemicals to the ecosystem for reuse.

What is happening in such an ecosystem? What connects the various parts together so that life is maintained? The answer lies in the two concepts discussed earlier in Section 4-2, namely, chemical recycling and energy flow. Life in an ecosystem is possible only when essential chemicals are recycled and energy flows through the ecosystem, as illustrated in Figure 4-4.

Using a highly complex photosynthetic process, green plants convert carbon dioxide and water into food molecules — carbo-

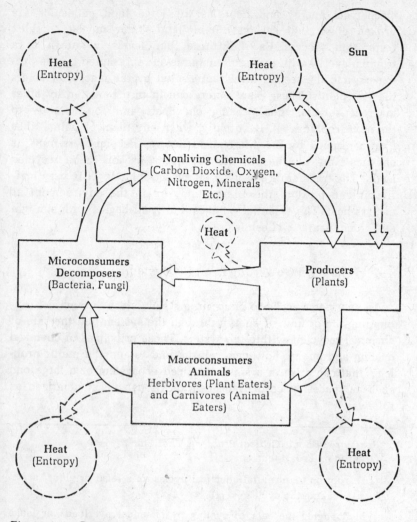

Figure 4–4 Components of an ecosystem showing chemical cycling (solid lines) and energy flow (dotted lines).

hydrates, fats, and proteins. In this process solar energy is transformed to chemical potential energy, or food energy. Some of this food energy is used by plants but much of it goes to other animals grazing on the plants. They transfer some of the chemicals to their bodies and convert some of the chemical, or food, energy into mechanical energy and heat, as the large food molecules are broken down into carbon dioxide and water in the complex respiration process. Each of these food levels is known as a trophic level — with the first trophic level represented by the producers, and the second level represented by the macroconsumers that eat plants. These plant eaters can in turn be eaten by other macroconsumers, thus passing chemicals and food energy to the next trophic level. Eventually, when any plant or animal dies it is consumed by the microconsumers, or decomposers, and its chemicals are returned to the air, water, or soil to be recycled again. The transfer of energy from each trophic level is very inefficient and most of the energy ends up in the environment as useless heat. The essential point is that it all begins with sunlight and green plants. All flesh is grass.

4–4   What Can Go Wrong in an Ecosystem?

An ecosystem seeks to maintain a steady state through controlling the rate of flow of energy through the system and the rate of chemical recycling within the system. These principles of chemical cycling and energy flow can help us understand the major problems that can arise in a small localized ecosystem or a large one such as spaceship earth. These problems can be summarized as follows:

Summary of Some Critical Problems That Can Occur in an Ecosystem

1. Disruption of essential chemical cycles on a local or global scale.
   a. Breaking the cycle.
   b. Changing the rate of cycling by chemical overloads or leaks in the cycle.

2. Disruption of energy flow on a local or global scale.

   a. Decreasing or increasing solar-energy input by changing the properties of the local or global atmosphere.

   b. Heat or entropy buildup in the environment due to too many passengers using too much energy — we can't ignore or repeal the Second Law of Thermodynamics.

One class of problems would involve disrupting one or more of the essential chemical cycles. Life depends not only on the existence of these cycles on a global and local scale but on the maintenance of a particular rate of cycling. For example, oxygen produced by photosynthesis is recycled about every 2000 years while carbon dioxide produced by respiration in cells is recycled about every 300 years. Trouble can therefore occur in one of three ways: (1) by breaking the cycle, (2) by altering the rate of cycling through overloading the cycle with chemicals at certain points, or (3) by allowing chemicals to leak out at some point in the cycle. These problems can occur on a localized scale (particularly in industrialized society) and perhaps eventually on a global scale so that the entire life-support system or at least the quality of life for everyone is threatened. Hopefully, those of us in a "throwaway society" are finally beginning to realize that on a finite spaceship you can't really throw anything away — there is no "away." An understanding of the chemical recycling processes in nature can enable us to preserve these cycles and guide us in recovering and recycling some of the valuable chemicals that we have been discarding or tying up in nonuseful forms.

A second class of problems involves disrupting the flow of energy through the spaceship. Our atmosphere regulates the flow of solar energy into the ship and the radiation of heat back into space. If its composition is changed significantly then too much or too little energy would be let in or out and the atmosphere might gradually heat up or cool down. It has been estimated that a 2°C rise in average atmospheric temperature would cause major changes in global weather patterns and a 3° rise could melt the polar ice caps, thus flooding much of the world. On the other hand, a 2 to 3°C drop in the average atmospheric temperature could produce a new ice age.[1]

Excessive heat or entropy buildup inside the ship can also occur through man's activities, as a consequence of the Second Law of Thermodynamics. As we saw in the last chapter (See Section 3-3),

---

[1] Report of the Study of Critical Environmental Problems (SCEP), *Man's Impact on the Global Environment,* The MIT Press: Cambridge, Mass., 1970, p. 10, 46-43, 82-96; and Report of the Study of Man's Impact on Climate (SMIC), *Inadvertent Climate Modification,* The MIT Press: Cambridge, Mass.: 1971, p. 124-130, 238-9.

essentially all of man's activities add heat to the atmosphere, and adding more and more passengers who use more and more energy ultimately could result in overheating, first on a local scale (around cities) and eventually on a global scale.[2]

4–5 The Carbon and Oxygen Cycles

The bulk of living matter is made up of four chemical elements — carbon, hydrogen, oxygen, and nitrogen. For life to continue we have seen that these critical elements must move in interconnected chemical cycles throughout the biosphere. Although there are a number of important biogeochemical cycles, we shall look at three representative ones: the carbon, oxygen, and nitrogen cycles.[3]

Carbon is the basic building-block element of all large organic molecules necessary for life. From a chemical standpoint all life on earth is based primarily on carbon compounds. The source of carbon for plants and animals is the carbon dioxide that makes up about 0.03 percent of our atmosphere and the CO_2 dissolved in the waters that cover two-thirds of the earth.

As shown in Figure 4-5 carbon undergoes a complete cycle. It moves from CO_2 in the air and water to plants through photosynthesis, and from there through the food chain to plant-eating animals (herbivores) and flesh-eating animals (carnivores). At each step part of the carbon stored in complex food molecules is broken down to provide energy for the organism and returned to the air and water as CO_2 by the process of cellular respiration. The remaining carbon is also returned to the air and water when the plant or animal eventually dies and is broken down into CO_2 by the bacteria and fungi that decompose organic matter. While the carbon is used over and over again, we see in Figure 4-5 that

---

[2] More detailed discussions of whether or not these energy-flow problems will become serious are found in Section 4-5 of this chapter and in Section 7-4 of Chapter 7.

[3] For more details on these and other chemical cycles see the September, 1970 issue of the *Scientific American,* a superb issue devoted entirely to a discussion of the biosphere. It also has been published by W. H. Freeman & Co. as a separate book entitled *The Biosphere.*

the solar energy used to drive the cycle is converted first to chemical energy in the chemical bonds in the larger carbon containing molecules, and then primarily to heat in the atmosphere when the chemical energy is released as the molecules are broken down. This heat energy then flows back into space.

The oxygen cycle is interdependent with the carbon cycle. When CO_2 and H_2O are used in photosynthesis by plants, O_2 is produced, and it is then converted back to H_2O and CO_2 by respiration in plant and animal cells.

Photosynthesis [4]

$$\text{carbon dioxide} + \text{water} \xrightarrow[\text{energy}]{\text{solar}} \text{large organic molecules} + \text{oxygen}$$

$$CO_2 + H_2O \xrightarrow[\text{energy}]{\text{solar}} \text{large organic molecules} + O_2$$

Cellular Respiration [4]

$$\text{large organic molecules} + \text{oxygen} \longrightarrow \text{carbon dioxide} + \text{water} + \text{energy}$$

$$\text{large organic molecules} + O_2 \longrightarrow CO_2 + H_2O + \text{energy}$$

A greatly simplified version of the carbon and oxygen cycle is shown in Figure 4-5. By stripping away some of the details, we can see more clearly how carbon and oxygen are cycled while energy from the sun flows through the biosphere and is degraded to less useful forms in the process. The energy is converted from solar energy $\longrightarrow$ chemical energy $\longrightarrow$ heat. Plants convert the solar energy to chemical energy through photosynthesis. Some of this chemical energy is used by the plant or animal in respiration and other processes necessary for life. Because of the Second Law of Thermodynamics, the efficiency of energy conversion at each step

---

[4] The chemical reactions listed under photosynthesis and respiration are not meant to imply that these chemicals react directly and simply to produce the products. The detailed mechanisms of photosynthesis and respiraton are complex and each involves a large number of interconnected chemical reactions.

is very low and most of it ends up as essentially useless heat energy in the atmosphere.

As shown in Figure 4-5, all of the carbon is not immediately recycled by the photosynthesis-respiration cycle in living organisms. In the course of millions of years part of the carbon from decayed plants and animals has been temporarily removed from the normal carbon cycling and incorporated by geological processes into the earth's crust as fossil or carbon fuels (coal, natural gas, and oil) or as carbonate rock formations (such as limestone and coral reefs). These fossil fuels and rock deposits represent a temporary storage of carbon and solar energy in concentrated form. As man burns, or combusts, these fossil fuels this carbon is returned to the carbon cycle as CO_2 and the solar energy temporarily stored as chemical energy is released back into the atmosphere as heat.

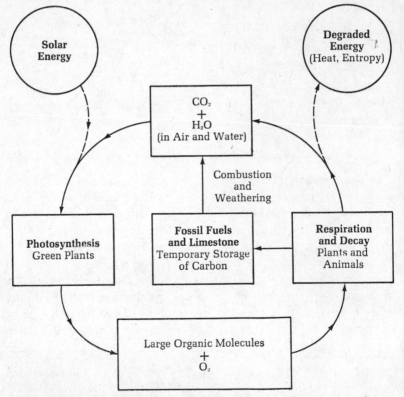

Figure 4–5 Simplified version of the carbon and oxygen cycles in the biosphere.

Since these fossil fuels took millions and millions of years to form, we must consider them as nonrenewable resources; once used this concentrated form of useful energy will no longer be available. The carbon tied up in carbonate rock formations is also eventually returned to the carbon cycle as CO_2 as these rocks undergo very slow dissolution by weathering.

Now man has the potential to disrupt the carbon cycle on a local or global level. Since the industrial revolution we have been using fossil fuels at an increasing rate and thus releasing carbon back into the atmosphere as carbon dioxide, CO_2, and carbon monoxide, CO. Of course plants and animals and other natural processes release CO_2 into the atmosphere as part of the carbon cycle; but there is concern that man might eventually overload the natural carbon cycle. Our atmosphere has evolved over millions of years by the action of plants and animals. As a result of this it contains a balance of gases such as N_2, O_2, CO_2, and H_2O that supports life as we know it. Upsetting our present steady state, by releasing too much CO_2 into the atmosphere over a relatively short period of time (several hundred years), could have serious consequences.

During the last 100 years the carbon dioxide, CO_2, content of our atmosphere has risen almost 10 percent because of the burning of fossil fuels, and the rate is increasing. As a result, the CO_2 content of the atmosphere has increased at 0.2 percent each year since 1958. At this rate, by the year 2000 the CO_2 content would be 25 percent higher than 1958 levels.

It is believed by some that this rise in CO_2 content could eventually produce what is known as the "greenhouse effect." The CO_2 admits radiant energy from the sun into the atmosphere, but it prevents some lower energy radiation (heat) from escaping back into space. As CO_2 builds up there could be a gradual warming of the earth's atmosphere, perhaps as much as $0.5°C$ by the year 2000. A rise of only 2 to $3°C$ could cause the Antarctic ice sheet to melt or slip into the ocean, thus raising the sea level by anywhere from 100 to 400 feet, over a long period of years.[5] Such a

---

[5] See the references in the Footnote on pages 67 and 72 and Report of the Environmental Pollution Panel President's Science Advisory Committee, *Restoring the Quality of the Environment*, U.S. Government Printing Office, Washington, D.C., 1965 p. 119-124.

rise in the sea level would put most of the world's major cities under water — hardly a desirable "solution" to the overpopulation problem.

Such projections, however, are quite uncertain because we know so very little about our atmosphere. There is considerable debate in the scientific community as to whether this or other processes are occurring as well as debate on their long-term effects. Indeed, some project that the atmosphere may be cooling rather than heating because of increased amounts of dust from volcanoes and wind storms coupled with the dust, soot, and other particulate matter man is pouring into the atmosphere. It is hypothesized that a rise in particulate matter in the atmosphere would reflect or absorb some of the incoming solar radiation and thus prevent some of it from getting through the atmosphere, thus producing a cooling effect and possibly a new ice age. Such effects are probably not immediate dangers, but on a long-range basis they could be most serious. The important point is that we don't really know enough to predict what might happen — but we do know that for the first time man now has the potential to bring about changes in atmospheric balance on a local (for example, around a city) and a global scale.[6] A recent authoritative study[7] of these and other major environmental problems stated:

"Although we conclude that the probability of direct climate change in this century resulting from CO_2 is small, we stress that the long-term potential consequences of CO_2 effects on the climate or of societal reaction to such threats are so serious that much more must be learned about future trends of climate change."

---

[6] The land investor who is cynical about whether man will really clean up his "environmental mess" in time might purchase land in the midwest. It could then be used as beachfront property or as a cross-country ski resort, depending on whether we enter a new ice age or return to Noah's ark.

[7] Report of the Study of Critical Environmental Problems, *Man's Impact on the Global Environment,* The MIT Press, 1970 (paperback). An excellent and readable summary of environmental problems by teams of prominent scientists. An additional source is *Global Effects of Environmental Pollution,* S. F. Singer (ed.), Springer-Verlag, New York, Inc., 1970.

We can also potentially upset the oxygen and carbon cycles by decreasing photosynthetic activity through continuing elimination of plants and trees. In the United States we are bulldozing, chopping, and paving over our land with asphalt and concrete at an alarming rate — the equivalent to paving over the state of Rhode Island every six months.

We usually think of the familiar green plants and trees as carrying out all photosynthesis and providing our oxygen, but at least one-third [8] of all photosynthesis is carried out by the "grass of the sea," tiny microscopic plants called phytoplankton found floating in our oceans, rivers, and lakes. Man may already be upsetting the ecological balance in many of our water ecosystems. Pollution of the world's oceans is one of our most serious problems and it is projected to increase seven fold before the year 2000. We are presently dumping over 500,000 different man-made chemicals into our oceans, rivers, and lakes; and only a handful have been tested to determine their effect on photosynthesis in phytoplankton.

Does this mean that we are about to run out of oxygen as many horror stories in the popular press have indicated? Fortunately, recent calculations [9] indicate that we are in no real danger of running out of oxygen from these intrusions into the carbon and oxygen cycles. The danger lies more in upsetting the much needed food-producing capacity of our land and oceans by removing vegetation and disrupting natural checks and balances between various living organisms in land and water systems.[10] More and more prime farm land is taken over by urbanization. As land is cleared much of the valuable nutrients are washed away into water systems — thus providing a nutrient leak on the land and frequently a nutrient overload in our rivers and lakes. It is these intrusions into the vital chemical cycles that most concern us.

---

[8] Some references indicate that about 70% of photosynthesis is carried out by plants in the oceans, rivers and lakes, because they cover 70% of the surface of the planet. However, the total mass of sea plants is much less than that of land plants and Robert Whittaker has calculated that land plants produce the larger share of oxygen.

[9] W. S. Broecker, *Science, 168*, 1537 (1970).

[10] For a startling scenario showing what could happen to the oceans and to man if he continues to disrupt the ocean ecosystem, see the article entitled "Eco-Catastrophe!" by Dr. Paul Ehrlich, Professor of Biology, Stanford University, in *Eco-Catastrophe*, Canfield Press (Harper & Row, Publishers), 1970.

Nitrogen is another element required by all living organisms. Indeed it occupies a special place in terms of human life because it is a sensitive indicator of the quality of health in humans. Nitrogen deprivation is the first sign of poverty and famine; a lack of nitrogen primarily in the form of protein quickly leads to a weakened condition and poor health. Nitrogen is a key element in essential molecules such as proteins, nucleic acids, enzymes, vitamins, and hormones. As we shall see later, world hunger is primarily protein hunger and, as the human population continues to grow, nitrogen will become the critical element in attempting to prevent catastrophic famine.

Figures 4-4 and 4-6 can be used to help us see how nitrogen is recycled. Nitrogen is very abundant in the form of N_2 gas, which makes up about 80 percent of our atmosphere. Unfortunately this form of nitrogen cannot be used by most organisms. With the aid of certain bacteria, a very small number of plants can convert, or

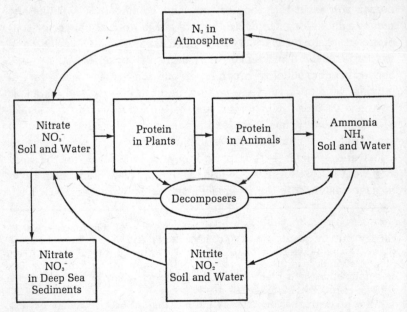

Figure 4–6   Greatly simplified version of the nitrogen cycle. Conversions from one form of nitrogen to another are each carried out by special types of bacteria.

fix, N_2 directly into organic nitrogen, primarily in the form of proteins. Most of the nitrogen in living organisms does not enter directly from the atmosphere. Instead, another group of bacteria in the soil and water can convert gaseous nitrogen, N_2, to inorganic nitrogen in the form of nitrate, or NO_3^-. Plants then obtain this nitrate as a nutrient from the soil or water and convert it to organic nitrogen, primarily in the form of nucleic acids and protein. Since nitrogen is also essential for photosynthesis, the amount of nitrate in the soil can regulate crop growth, thus explaining why the addition of artificial nitrate fertilizer can give greater yields.

When animals (herbivores) eat the plants, some of the organic nitrogen is transferred to these animals and eventually to other animals that feed upon these animals. When the plants and animals die, their organic nitrogen is then converted by decomposers to inorganic nitrogen in the form of ammonia, or NH_3, which is converted by another group of bacteria into another form of inorganic nitrogen, nitrite, NO_2^-. The ammonia, NH_3, can also be converted to atmospheric nitrogen, N_2. Another group of bacteria can convert the nitrite, NO_2^-, back to nitrate, NO_3^-, which can be taken up again by plants to begin the cycle again. Some nitrogen is lost from the cycle when soluble nitrates are washed from the soil and deposited as deep-sea sediments.

4–7 Disrupting the Nitrogen Cycle

Man's activities can now upset the nitrogen cycle. The danger here apparently is not in disrupting the cycle on a global scale but in upsetting it at the local level in a particular lake or soil system.

For example, consider what is happening to the natural nitrogen content in much of the soil in industrialized nations. Most of the nitrogen in the soil is contained in a complex mixture of organic and inorganic nitrogen-containing compounds, called humus. If the nitrogen cycle in the soil is functioning normally, very little nitrogen is lost, or washed, from the soil into nearby rivers or lakes and the fertility of the soil is maintained. However, if land is not planted properly or if it is overfarmed, much of this natural soil nitrogen can be lost by surface runoff; a nutrient leak occurs and nitrogen, primarily in the form of nitrate (NO_3^-), is transferred from the soil to nearby water systems. In addition to this leaching, or leakage, whenever there is harvesting, nitrogen is also removed. To maintain fertility it must be replaced by natural or artificial means. When we consider that it may take up to 500 years to build an inch of topsoil, we can appreciate the loss in fertility in American farms each year when over 2-billion tons of sediment are washed away by rain and irrigation.

As the land has been misused and slowly depleted of nutrients by continued use, we have been able to maintain or even increase crop yields by adding artificial, or man-made, nitrogen in the form of inorganic fertilizers — as contrasted with organic fertilizers, provided naturally by waste and decay from plants and animals. Organic fertilizer cannot be used by plants until it is converted to inorganic nutrients by soil bacteria.

Unfortunately, overloading a soil with inorganic fertilizer apparently upsets the homeostatic balance of this crucial bacterial action. In the United States the use of inorganic chemical fertilizer has grown rapidly since World War II, increasing some 14-fold in the past 25 years. This has allowed us to grow more food, but at the same time it is causing some serious problems. Unfortunately, when inorganic nitrogen fertilizer is used the amount of natural organic nitrogen in the soil can drop and the efficiency of the transfer of the nitrate from the soil to the plant can decrease. This means that some of the nitrate in the soil is not used and can be washed off into nearby streams or lost in other forms of nitrogen (for example, NH_3) to the atmosphere. Ironically, as a result of the extensive use of inorganic nitrogen fertilizer, a nitrogen nutrient leak has developed in many heavily farmed areas. The natural nitrogen content of the soil has been depleted while nearby water systems have become overloaded with excess nitrogen. This can result in a kind of "chemical vicious circle," where more and more fertilizer must be added as the soil becomes poorer and poorer and our water systems become more and more overburdened with too much nitrate.

What can excess nitrate or other nutrients (for example, phosphate) do to an aquatic ecosystem, such as a lake? Some chemicals and nutrients naturally run off of the land into a lake and as a result a lake becomes shallower over time as sediment builds up over the years. This natural aging process of nutrient enrichment and sedimentation is called eutrophication. All lakes naturally age and eventually "die." When man increases soil erosion or introduces excess quantities of sewage, industrial waste, or fertilizer runoff, he can greatly accelerate the aging of the lake. This form of man-made eutrophication is called cultural eutrophication. The premature aging and "partial death" of Lake Erie is a good example of man's intervention in the natural chemical cycles. Again, we know relatively little about what happens in complex aquatic and soil ecosystems. Different lakes and soil systems have different characteristics and problems, but a crude general picture is emerging.[11]

Plant life in a lake requires a balanced input of nitrates (and phosphates) as food, or nutrients. When plants or animals die or when organic matter or waste is washed or dumped into a lake, bacteria decompose the organic matter and return it to the lake as nitrate, phosphate, and other minerals that can be used to support plant and animal life. The lake is cleansed and life is maintained by the nitrogen cycle (see Figure 4–6). This magnificent cleansing and nutrient cycle works well as long as it is not too heavily stressed. If the lake is overloaded by excess nitrates and phosphates, the entire nitrogen cycle and eventually the carbon and oxygen cycles can be disrupted on a local scale; with excess plant nutrient present, an explosive growth of plants, particularly algae, may occur. The resulting "algal blooms" cannot be supported for long and they soon die, overburdening the water with dead organic matter. The decomposing bacteria break down this dead matter by oxidation and in the process deplete the oxygen content of the water. If the process of overfertilization continues, the aquatic ecosystem has less ability to support fish and other aquatic life that require oxygen. As they die, this further overloads the system with excess dead organic matter, the oxygen content falls even further, the life sustaining and purification

---

[11] A more detailed discussion of eutrophication can be found in the following refernces: 1. State of California, The Resources Agency, *Eutrophication — A Review,* Publication No. 34, State Water Quality Control Board, Sacramento, Calif., 1967; 2. National Academy of Sciences, *Eutrophication: Causes, Consequences, and Correctives,* 1969; 3. S. F. Singer (ed.), *Global Effects of Environmental Pollution,* Springer-Verlag, New York, Inc., 1970. See Part II, pp. 67-110. 4. N. C. Brady (ed.), *Agriculture and the Quality of Our Environment,* American Association for the Advancement of Science, 1967 (see especially pp. 163-220).

system collapses or is impaired, and the water becomes foul.

Unfortunately, in a modern industrialized society like the United States, there are many sources of nitrates and phosphates that can potentially overload many of our lakes. The "premature aging" of Lake Erie may be merely an early warning system. Some of the major man-caused sources of nitrates and phosphates are (1) *inorganic-fertilizer* runoff, (2) *municipal sewage-treatment plants,* (3) *animal-feedlot practices* that produce massive amounts of animal wastes by concentrating thousands or hundreds of thousands of animals in a "livestock factory," (4) *nitrogen-oxide emission* from the internal-combustion engine, and (5) *phosphates found in most synthetic detergents.* All of these can impinge simultaneously on a lake ecosystem to cause a massive nutrient overload and disruption of the natural rate of chemical cycling, as shown in Figure 4-7.

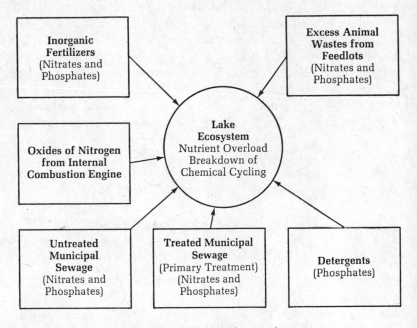

Figure 4–7 Sources of nutrient overloading and premature eutrophication of a lake in an industrialized society.

Obviously this process can be accelerated as the country increases its overall population along with increased industrialization and population concentration in areas around lakes (for example, the Great Lakes which contain 20 percent of all the fresh water on the earth.)[12] Furthermore, as population grows, more and more fertilizer must be used to maintain high yields of food and more and more animal wastes accumulate from our efficient feedlot system for growing more livestock for the population. In the United States animal wastes produced each year amount to 2-billion tons— enough each year to fill a train reaching from here to the moon and halfway back and equivalent to the human waste produced by 2-billion people. In other words, animals in the United States produce 10 times more waste than the entire U.S. population so that we can have a meat-based diet. If the excess animal wastes were used as organic fertilizer, we could eliminate some of the need for inorganic fertilizer. Unfortunately, the problem at present is primarily economic rather than technological; inorganic fertilizer is relatively cheap. If we paid the real cost for inorganic fertilizers, including their devastating impact on our environment, then the use of organic fertilizer would again become economically feasible.

Ironically, as we spend more and more money in building primary sewage-treatment plants for our towns and cities, they can also add excess nitrates and phosphates to aquatic ecosystems and we will eventually be forced to go to much more expensive tertiary treatment plants that remove nitrates and phosphates.

The automobile, or more correctly the internal-combustion engine, is normally thought of in terms of air pollution, but it is also a contributor to nitrate water pollution. Large cities generally fall into one of two basic air-pollution classes — the brown-air cities and the gray-air cities. Brown-air cities, like Los Angeles, are relatively young cities, where the main source of air pollution is the internal- (or infernal-) combustion engine in the automobile. Every automobile spews several hundred different compounds into the air. One of these compounds is gaseous nitric oxide, NO, which is formed in the engine at high temperatures by the reaction of nitrogen, N_2, and oxygen, O_2, in the air used to burn the fuel. Nitric

---

[12] Something similar to eutrophication can also occur in slow-flowing rivers and along ocean coastlines. See for example, J. Monster and T. Reimer, "Nitrogen, Phosphorus, and Eutrophication in the Coastal Marine Environment" *Science*, 171, 1008 (1971).

oxide, NO, is relatively harmless but it can react with oxygen, O_2, in the air to form nitrogen dioxide, NO_2, a yellow-brown poisonous gas that produces the brown haze over car-oriented cities, such as Los Angeles. Nitrogen dioxide may be harmful to the lungs. Even more serious is the fact that in the presence of sunlight it combines with carbon-hydrogen compounds (hydrocarbons), also emitted in auto exhausts, to form a whole new brew of chemicals. This mixture, called photochemical smog, contains chemicals that irritate the eyes and damage vegetation. Furthermore the nitrogen dioxide can dissolve in water and be converted to nitrate, thus adding to the nitrate water-pollution problem. To reduce this form of air and water pollution to a satisfactory level, it seems likely that the internal-combustion engine must be replaced.

Emission control devices now installed on cars do a poor job of reducing oxides of nitrogen and may actually increase their concentration. Many experts argue that emission control devices provide only a temporary solution, which buys us a little time (perhaps 5-10 years) to find a replacement for the internal-combustion engine. If, over a period of years, these devices reduce all dangerous air pollutants, on the average, by 50 percent and during the same time the number of cars doubles (as projected), then air-pollution levels will return to present levels and even rise again as more cars are added.

The second type of city, the gray-air city, is an older city, such as New York, Chicago, and London, that depends heavily on the burning of coal or oil for heating, manufacturing, and electric-power generation. This burning normally produces two major air pollutants: (1) particulates (dust and soot), which give the air over such cities its gray cast, and (2) sulfur dioxide, one of the most dangerous pollutants in our air. Coal and oil usually are contaminated with sulfur, S, and when they are burned, the sulfur combines with the oxygen of the air to produce sulfur-dioxide gas, SO_2. The level of sulfur dioxide in our air, already critical, is expected to double in the next 20 years. It can damage plants, dissolve marble and concrete, and eat away iron and steel, not to mention what it does to delicate lung tissue. Exposure for 24 hours to only 0.2 parts per million of SO_2, with particulate matter also present in the air, is considered to be a serious health hazard. The SO_2 is also connected to the nitrogen-dioxide problem from the automobile. SO_2 can react with oxygen, O_2, in the air to produce sulfur-trioxide gas, SO_3, which when breathed can react with water to produce droplets of sulfuric acid on lung tissue. Unfortunately, traces of nitrogen dioxide, NO_2, in the air can serve as a catalyst to increase the rate of oxidation of SO_2 to SO_3.

Thus, we can begin to see that our air-pollution problem can be connected to another, and in some cases they in turn may be connected to a water-pollution problem. We can never do one thing to an ecosystem; the problems and solutions are complex, not simple. How can we minimize or reduce the overfertilization of lakes, such as Lake Erie? No one really knows at this point. Obviously, reducing overall population and population concentration would help decrease inorganic fertilizer use, animal wastes, automobiles, detergents, and sewage-treatment plants. In addition, we might ban or reduce certain pollutants or use animal waste and municipal sewage as organic fertilizer instead of making more and more inorganic fertilizer as summarized in Figure 4-8. For example we might put research efforts on developing new technologies

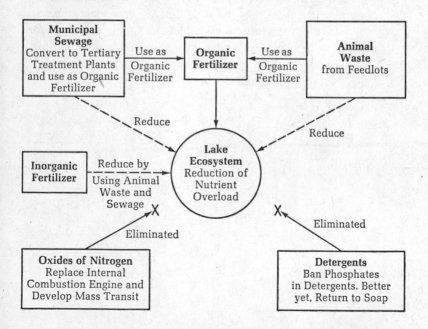

Figure 4–8 A possible scheme for reducing nutirent overload coupled with a reduction in overall demand by reducing population and population density.

that could transport sewage and garbage to agricultural areas, thus completing rather than disrupting our natural ecological cycles. To make any significant progress we must deal with all of the variables in figure 4-8, not just one, and it will be expensive. It is easier and cheaper to get into trouble than it is to get out of it.

We have seen that our life-support system depends on a magnificent system of chemical cycling and energy flow that developed during millions of years of evolution. We are now at a unique and unprecedented crossroads in the history of mankind. For the first time we have the capacity to destroy or seriously impair our life-support system, particularly at the localized level, and global disruptions could occur within the next 100 to 150 years if we continue on our present path of more and more people consuming more and more resources.

I am tired of hearing that man is on his way to extinction, along with most other forms of life. My own view of man suggests that something worse than extinction is in store for us. It is not man as a species the ecological crisis threatens to destroy but the quality of human life, the attributes that make human life different from animal life.

René Dubos

5

Preserving Stability in Our Life-Support System

5–1 A Short Course in Cybernetics

We learned earlier that the most important principle of ecology is that in a finite closed system everything is connected to everything; everything in the system ultimately feeds back through the system upon itself. All parts of the ecosystem are affected by a major change in any other part, or subsystem.

It is precisely this interconnectedness between a complex array of parts that preserves the overall system. The natural tendency of any organism, group of organisms, or ecosystem is to maintain a balanced, or steady, state despite environmental changes, stresses, and shocks.

What we are really saying is that an organism or ecosystem can be viewed as a cybernetic system. A cybernetic system is one that maintains control by feeding information back into the system to alter it as environmental conditions change— a self-regulating system based on information feedback. The ecosystems that make up our life-support system (the biosphere) form a giant and elaborate set of cybernetic systems linked together by information feedback in order to preserve overall stability.

One of the simplest cybernetic systems is a thermostat. A sensor monitors the room temperature and feeds this information back to a switch which cuts the furnace on or off. In the case of the thermostat a rise in room temperature is converted into information to cause the system to change in the opposite direction to lower the temperature. This type of information flow is known as <u>negative feedback</u>. A second form of feedback, known as <u>positive feedback</u>, causes the system to respond by changing in the same direction. The basic components of a simple feedback loop system are a sensor to monitor the environment, a comparator to compare the actual value with the desired value of whatever is being controlled, and an effector for bringing about the desired change, as summarized in Figure 5-1.

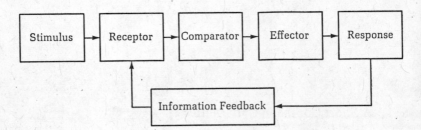

Figure 5–1   Generalized diagram of a simple cybernetic system.

A good example of cybernetic control in living organisms is the method by which our bodies are kept within a few degrees of the normal body temperature of 98.6°F. If the temperature of our environment rises, sensory devices detect this, send a message to the brain (our comparator), and the brain in turn activates an effector mechanism to cause sweating. The excreted water evaporates and removes heat from the skin. The sensors feed this new information back (negative feedback) to decrease or stop the sweating process. On the other hand, if the environment is too cold, a similar mechanism causes sweating to stop, decreases blood flow, and may activate a shivering or exercise mechanism so that the body will produce more heat.

Any cybernetic, or feedback, system can be overloaded. When environmental conditions exceed the operating limits of the system, it goes out of control as runaway feedback takes over. For example, the temperature can become so hot or cold that our thermostatic mechanism fails and we suffer heat stroke or freeze to death. In order to maintain stability in an organism or in an ecosystem a number of variables such as body temperature, blood pressure, body fluid content, and so on must be controlled within certain values. In cybernetic language we say they must be controlled so that they fluctuate around a <u>homeostatic plateau</u>, that is, a steady state near the desired value, as shown in Figure 5-2.

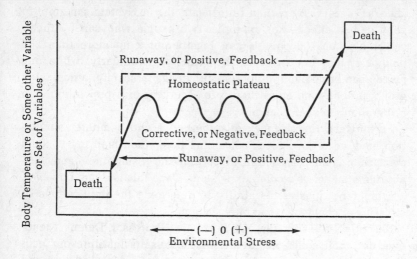

Figure 5–2 The homeostatic plateau. When values of a particular property in an organism or ecosystem exceed the working limits of the system, it goes out of control.

In organisms and in ecosystems the situation is far more complex than the simple feedback loop pictured in Figure 5-1. In nature we have thousands and even millions of different feedback loops all interconnected in a very complex manner.

One of our problems is that man is not very good at thinking and making correct predictions about what will happen in a complex cybernetic system. Yet all of our social, economic, and ecological systems are of this type. Man can make useful predictions only by using simple straight-line models that contain only a small number of variables. As he tries to apply this "model-T" thinking to complex social, governmental, and ecological cybernetic systems, his "common sense" or intuitive, solutions often make the situation worse in the long run. We are finding increasingly that the implications of a certain policy are often counterproductive, just the reverse of what we would intuitively expect.

Another way of looking at this difficulty is in terms of the idea of *synergy*. By linear thinking two plus two is four. But in a cybernetic system two variables may interact synergistically so that two plus two may be greater or less than four. That it is less than four means an ecosystem is resilient and can absorb rather severe shocks. That it is more than four means the ecosystem can amplify good or bad effects. For example, two people who can by themselves pick up 100 pounds can together pick up more than 200 pounds if they cooperate in the right way. Similarly, while one person can bring about only a small change in society, a dedicated group, probably no more than 3 to 5 percent of a population, can bring about radical change.

Fortunately, the sciences of cybernetics and computer simulation have been developed just at the time when man needs them most. Man is unsurpassed in discerning the assumptions and variables in a model of a complex system. Once this is done, however, a computer surpasses his ability to determine the implications of stressing or changing a complex system.

Recently Professor Jay W. Forrester, Professor Dennis Meadows, and their colleagues at the Massachusetts Institute of Technology have been applying computer simulation to modeling and making predictions about the world ecosystem. They have studied the cybernetic interaction of six major variables: pollution, population, capital investment, natural resources, food production, and quality of life.

A summary of this important work was presented by Jay Forrester in 1971 and by Dennis Meadows in 1972.[1] Figure 5-3, which has been adapted from their work, is a cybernetic diagram showing the interactions between the factors affecting the six major variables. This model was then simulated by the computer to make predictions. For example, we could ask what might happen to pollution, natural-resource depletion, capital investment, and food production if we cut population growth by 50 percent. Or, we might ask what would happen to the other variables if we cut pollution by 50 percent. Look at Figure 5-3 and see if you can come up with some answers. I think you can see why man is not capable of making predictions about complex cybernetic systems.

---

[1] J. W. Forrester, *World Dynamics*. Cambridge, Mass.: Wright-Allen Press, 1971 and D. H. Meadows, D. L. Meadows, et al. *The Limits of Growth: A Global Challenge*. New York: Universe Books, 1972.

In Chapter 7 we shall look more closely at some of the projections based on this world model. Figure 5-3 shows us two key factors for preserving stability in an ecosystem: (1) multiple-feedback loops and (2) a high degree of diversity. The greater the diversity of an ecosystem, that is, the greater the variety and interconnection between component parts, the greater its ability to withstand stress. Let us look at this diversity in terms of the biological species that make up our biosphere.

5–2 Preserving Ecological Diversity

Why should you thank a green plant, an alligator, or a hippopotamus today and every day? Why should we be concerned about preserving all of the diverse species of plant and animal life on this planet? The answer goes far beyond a desire to preserve beauty and unspoiled, or natural, areas, although these are very important reasons. We are now realizing that our very survival depends on preserving diversity and complexity in the earth's ecosystem, the biosphere. This vast network of chemical and biological interactions generates and preserves our soil and air and maintains the purity of our water. We have seen that interrupting the processes of energy flow and chemical cycling or changing the rate at which they occur can threaten the stability of our life-support process at the local and in the long run even at the global level.

But there is another reason for preserving plants and animals. They represent the biological capital provided by evolution. We are beginning to understand that *species diversity normally means ecosystem stability*. The more species present, the greater the possibility for adapting to changing conditions. We now recognize the importance of *the conservation of genetic information* — the idea that we ought to preserve every single species of life somewhere in its natural habitat because we presently have no way of knowing what animal or plant is now essential or may prove valuable or essential in the future. A living species is an irreplaceable resource; once extinct, it can never be recalled. Modern man has exterminated over 200 species of plants and animals in the last 150 years. Today over 500 others are on the danger list and the list is growing.

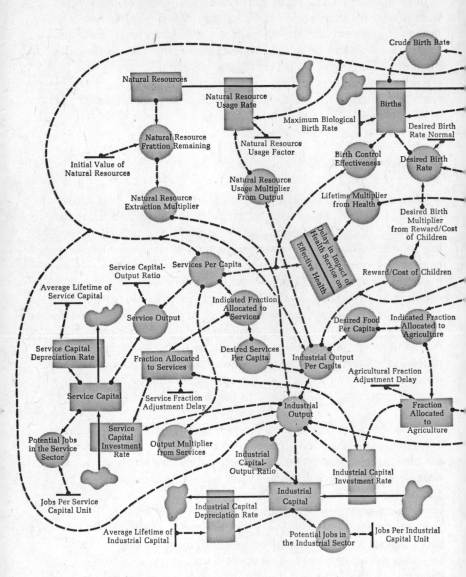

Figure 5–3 A cybernetic model for the world. The rectangles
represent the variable (population, pollution, and so on) while the
fire-extinguisher shapes representing rates (birth rate, death rate, etc.)
which affect the level of the variables. Circles are auxiliary factors that
strongly affect rates. The irregular cloud-like shapes represent

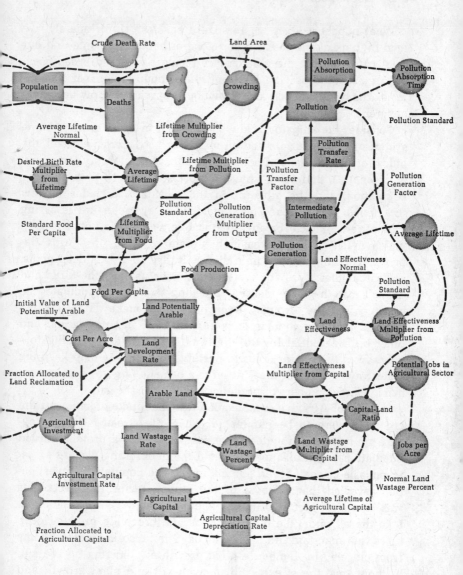

Crude Death Rate

Land Area

Population

Deaths

Crowding

Pollution Absorption

Pollution Absorption Time

Pollution

Pollution Standard

Average Lifetime Normal

Lifetime Multiplier from Crowding

Desired Birth Rate Multiplier from Lifetime

Lifetime Multiplier from Pollution

Average Lifetime

Pollution Transfer Rate

Pollution Transfer Factor

Pollution Generation Factor

Standard Food Per Capita

Lifetime Multiplier from Food

Pollution Standard

Pollution Generation Multiplier from Output

Intermediate Pollution

Pollution Generation

Average Lifetime

Food Production

Land Effectiveness Normal

Food Per Capita

Pollution Standard

Initial Value of Land Potentially Arable

Land Potentially Arable

Land Effectiveness

Land Effectiveness Multiplier from Pollution

Cost Per Acre

Land Development Rate

Fraction Allocated to Land Reclamation

Land Effectiveness Multiplier from Capital

Potential Jobs in Agricultural Sector

Arable Land

Capital-Land Ratio

Agricultural Investment

Land Wastage Rate

Land Wastage Percent

Land Wastage Multiplier from Capital

Jobs per Acre

Agricultural Capital Investment Rate

Normal Land Wastage Percent

Agricultural Capital

Average Lifetime of Agricultural Capital

Fraction Allocated to Agricultural Capital

Agricultural Capital Depreciation Rate

variables that are considered to be unimportant. (Source: This chart is based on the charts used by Forrester and Meadows. It was prepared by Nancy Montague of the World Future Society and appeared in *The Futurist*, August, 1971. Reproduced by permission of the World Future Society.)

What happens when we remove a species? Unfortunately, we tend to think of species as either good or bad and assume that our role is to wipe out the villains. We recklessly spread broad spectrum poisons across the land and place bounties on certain animals. The backlash from this "cowboy" approach is now becoming apparent.

Consider the alligator, a key species that in some areas is being systematically exterminated primarily by poachers who sell the hides for making fancy pocketbooks and shoes. In only ten years, between 1950 and 1960, Louisiana lost 90 percent of its alligator population, and the alligator in the Florida Everglades is now threatened. Who cares? The alligator is a key factor in preserving the entire ecological balance of the Everglades — a balance upon which much of the increasingly urbanized state of Florida depends. The alligator is a hole digger. In dry spells his deep pools, or "gator holes," provide water and a sanctuary so the birds and animals can begin a massive breeding cycle to repopulate the glades after the drought. Alligators also make large nesting mounds that are popular sites for nests of herons, egrets, and other birds essential for the life cycle in the glades. As alligators move from their gator holes to nesting mounds they help keep the waterways open, and they preserve a balance of game fish by consuming large numbers of predator fish, such as the gar.

In parts of Africa, it was decided that the hippopotamus and the crocodile were to be eliminated. Then the streams began clogging up, fish that provided essential protein for a protein-starved population began disappearing, and the debilitating disease schistosomiasis or snail fever, spread among the population. Investigation revealed that removal of the hippopotamus and crocodiles was a major factor bringing about these disastrous changes. Like the alligator, the hippopotamus and crocodile produce deep holes that maintain life in dry spells. They also keep the streams from clogging by removing plant growth and stirring up the silt. Without this, the streams fill up with silt and plant growth and become shallow and warm, an ideal situation for the massive breeding and spread of the snail that serves as a host for a parasitic flatworm causing schistosomiasis. This disease, which so far seems virtually incurable, makes a person so weak he can hardly hold up his arm. It has also spread into areas where man has expanded irrigation to feed more mouths. It thrives in warm shallow water streams and irrigation ditches and is now the world's most prevalent infectious disease.

Ironically, the Aswan Dam in Egypt, an engineering marvel, may prove to be an ecological disaster. In an effort to expand Egypt's arable land to increase food production for its growing population and to provide flood control and electric power, the nation built this magnificent structure. What has happened since it went into operation in 1964? First, the dam stopped the annual flow of silt to the Nile valley. This valley, once so fertile, now has to be treated with artificial fertilizer. To make matters worse, the loss of this nutrient-loaded silt has caused the collapse of the Mediterranean sardine-fishing industry, an important source of protein. The Egyptian sardine catch dropped from 18,000 tons in 1965 to a meager 500 tons in 1968.

But this is not all. The new irrigation system it provided is an ideal environment for the snails that spread the dreaded schistosomiasis. This disease now infects over one-half of the population in parts of Egypt. During the time it took to build the dam, the increase in Egyptian population surpassed the additional food it allows to be grown. We can never do only one thing in an ecosystem even with the best of intentions.

In Borneo, the World Health Organization sprayed large amounts of DDT to combat malaria by killing off mosquitoes. This greatly improved the quality of life, but other things began to happen. The DDT also poisoned house flies. Wonderful, you say. But the housefly was the favorite food of a tiny lizard called a gecko. The gecko gorged themselves on dead flies and died from the DDT. House cats then feasted on geckos and in turn were poisoned. With fewer cats, the rat population soared. The inhabitants of the island were then threatened by a new disease, sylvatic plague, carried by fleas on the rats. Fortunately, this tradeoff of sylvatic plague for malaria was averted when the Royal Air Force parachuted in a number of cats to control the rat population. Controls were imposed on the DDT spraying program until the ecological effects were minimized.

As if this wasn't enough the thatched roofs of the natives' houses began to fall in. The DDT also killed a number of wasps. Bravo, you say, they are always stinging people anyway. Unfortunately, these wasps fed on caterpillars. With their predators eliminated, the caterpillars had a population explosion and proceeded to munch their way through one of their favorite foods, the leaves that make up thatched roofs.

In the western part of the United States, official government policy called for the extermination of the coyote. In 1965 some $5,575,000 in Federal funds was spent in "predator control." Poison was spread widely to kill prairie dogs, wolves, foxes, and coyotes. Eagles, hawks, crows, and vultures fed on the carcasses and also died. As a result the rodent population, which the coyote and these other predators helped control, multiplied astronomically. The rodents attack the roots of prairie grass and destroy the range for sheep and cattle used to support man.

Back in 1883, plantation owners in Hawaii found that rats were destroying a good portion of their valuable sugar-cane crop. They had more ecological sense than we appear to have today; they decided to use natural biological control— the idea that nature already has built in predator-prey relationships that can in many cases be far more effective and less dangerous than chemical control with pesticides. They imported 36 pairs of mongooses, who feed on rodents.

Unfortunately, this ecologically sound idea backfired because they did not check on the feeding habits of the mongoose. The mongoose hunts by day and the rat hunts by night. Thus, for the most part they never met and both species continued to multiply. Now Hawaii has a mongoose problem during the day — they feed on chickens, ground nesting birds, and their eggs — and an even larger rat population at night. Each year the rats eat about 4½-million dollars worth of sugar cane.

Consider the biological heritage that we have left Viet Nam in our attempts to help its people. We have drenched over 5-million acres in South Viet Nam with herbicides.[2] More than one-third of its forest area has been sprayed with defoliants, one-half of the

---

[2] Chemical-Biological Warfare: U.S. Policies and International Effects. Hearings before the Subcommittee on National Security Policy and Scientific Developments of the House Committee on Foreign Affairs (1970); Hearings on Military Posture, House Armed Services Committee (1970); F. H. Tschirley *Science, 163,* 779 (1969) and E. W. Pfeiffer, *Science, 168,* 544 (1970), and A. W. Galston, "Warfare with Herbicides in Vietnam," in J. Harte and R. H. Socolow, *Patient Earth,* Holt, Rinehart & Winston; New York, 1971, p. 136-150.

country's mangrove forests killed off, and enough food destroyed by herbicides to feed 600,000 people for one year. The vegetation breaks down and nutrient minerals can leak out of the ecosystem to cause accelerated eutrophication. Insects and rodents are found all over the world but are usually kept in check by natural predator-prey relationships. By drenching the world with broad spectrum herbicides and insecticides, we can unbalance ecosystems throughout the world. Pesticides are a serious dilemma, being simultaneously knights and villains. DDT has saved perhaps millions of lives by reducing malaria and by cutting crop losses to provide more food for a starving world. But some of its ecologically harmful effects became known only after its use was worldwide. Many of the long-range effects of man-made chemicals on the ecosphere are not predictable, and even the relatively simple cases in this section are not completely understood.[3]

What should we do? Some use of chemical insecticides will be needed to grow more food, but only under strict control and supervision, and only for essential purposes. Fortunately, we are beginning to develop some, but not enough, *integrated, ecological approaches* to pest control that involve selective use of chemicals as well as natural predator-prey and other biological controls.

5–4 DDT In Your Fatty Tissue — Biological Magnification

Much to our dismay, we have found that some man-made chemicals cannot only be passed through the food chain towards man but in some cases their concentration is greatly increased, or magnified, in passing from one level to another. This process of concentration through the food chain is called biological amplification, or magnification.

In some cases, a tiny amount of a chemical such as DDT, measured in the soil in terms of parts per billion (ppb[4]) or even less,

---

[3] For information on other ecological backlashes see Favor, M. T. and Milton, J. (eds.), "The Unforeseen International Ecologic Boomerang," *American Naturalist, 78,* 42-72 (1969), and J. P. Milton and M. T. Favor, *The Careless Technology.* New York: Natural History Press, 1971.

[4] A part per billion is the equivalent of one ounce of alcohol in 7,530,000 gallons of water.

can be concentrated, or magnified, by a factor of hundreds of thousands or even millions as it makes its way up the food chain from plants toward animals like man. For example, on Long Island Sound some mosquito-infested marshes were sprayed with DDT. Since DDT is almost insoluble in water, its concentration in the surrounding water was measured and found to be very safe .000003 parts per million (ppm), or 3 parts per trillion (ppt). Zooplankton, at a higher food level, very quickly magnified this by a factor of about 10,000 to levels of DDT of 0.04 parts per million (ppm). It then built up further to about 0.5 ppm in the flesh of plankton-eating fish, then to 2.0 ppm in larger fish that ate the smaller fish. Finally, it was found in amounts as high as 25 ppm in the birds at the top of the chain who ate the larger fish. Of course, man also eats these larger fish. In other words, DDT was magnified by a factor of some 10 million over its original concentration, as summarized in Figure 5-4.

Some local officials proudly report that their public water supplies contain DDT only in parts per billion or parts per trillion. It is precisely because of this minute solubility of DDT in water and its large solubility in fatty tissue that it can be concentrated up the food chain toward man. On an average, each of us carries about 12 parts per million of DDT in our fatty tissues. Frankly, we have no idea what long-term effect, if any, this will have. We are carrying out a gigantic chemical experiment on the human race and we don't know when, how, or if the results will show up in future generations. There is no way to stop this experiment because DDT, which now covers the globe, is persistent — it breaks down slowly. Half of the millions of tons already in our environment will still be around ten years from now and half of that will still be around ten years later and so on.

Pesticides such as DDT help but also threaten us. They tend to reduce stability by simplifying the ecosystem, reducing important species susceptible to these nerve poisons. Second, they affect us directly by appearing in the large concentrations in our bodies and those of other animals at the top of the food chain. DDT is only one of thousands of man-made chemicals introduced into our environment. All are not magnified up the food chain; but those that are persistent (have long chemical lives) and are soluble in fat, like DDT, will most assuredly make their way into our bodies.

We have recently discovered that a group of chemicals sim-

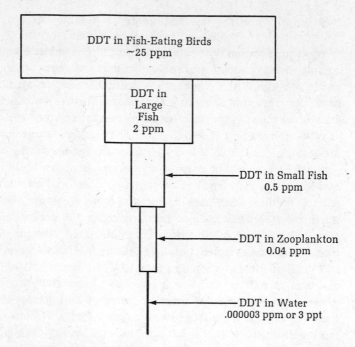

Figure 5–4 Concentrations of DDT magnified up the levels of a food chain on Long Island Sound. Total magnification factor is approximately 10-million times.

ilar to DDT — called the polychlorinated biphenyls, or *PCB* — have made their way up the food chain and, like DDT, are found worldwide in fish, chickens, birds, and many plant and animal species in the Atlantic Ocean. Again we don't yet know its long-term effect on man, but PCB like DDT is simplifying the eco-system structure by killing other species, shrimp and wild birds. If PCB compounds turn out to be harmful to man, this may be a much worse crisis than DDT, because PCB compounds are used in vast amounts in an array of products, including plastics, rubber, paints, and hydraulic fluid. It cannot be destroyed by incineration. It can enter the body through breathing or food, or it can pass directly through the skin. It is even more long lasting than DDT, although it is much less toxic than DDT. Again, much of its usefulness to industry lies in its long chemical life, or stability, and its solubility in oil or fat — the ideal characteristics for concentration up the food chain. Again we don't know what, if any, effect it will have in the long run. We are a gambling species.

What then is man doing to this essential ecological diversity and complexity? We attempt to rearrange nature to support immediate needs. We *simplify the ecosystem* so that we can control it. Paradoxically, this threatens our long-range survival by making the ecosystem more vulnerable to the very stresses we are imposing.

Without realizing it, we have linked much of our productive technological society to features that are incompatible with preserving the stability of our life-support system. We bulldoze fields and forests of thousands of interrelated plant and animal species, and cover them with asphalt for a shopping center, highway, or other form of urbanization. Farming, once diversified, now consists primarily of monocultures, that is, single crops of wheat, rice, or corn covering vast areas as far as the eye can see. Because of a lack of diversity, single crops must be supported by massive and ever-increasing doses of man-made chemical fertilizers, much of which washes into our lakes and streams and threatens to overload and disrupt the nitrogen and oxygen cycles. Because a monoculture crop can be wiped out rather easily by only a single species of insect, we attempt to protect it with more and stronger pesticides in a continually escalating form of chemical warfare rather than in using or developing biological pest controls. As the insects quickly breed resistance that we couldn't match even in several hundred-million years of additional evolution, some of these same poisons are magnified up the food chain to accumulate in the high concentrations in our bodies.

This is not to suggest that all of these practices are bad and that we shouldn't and won't keep on simplifying parts of our ecosystem. If we gave up modern agriculture, most of us would starve. We must do some simplification to survive, but our problem is twofold. First, we don't know which parts are really essential, and we don't know which of the man-made chemicals will be harmful in the long run. Furthermore, the idea that diversity always leads to stability can be carried too far. There are many different types of complexity in an ecosystem [5] and ecologists are not sure they all provide stability. The point is we know very little about ecosystems.

---

[5] For a more detailed discussion of this point see W. W. Murdoch, "Ecological Systems," p. 20-26 in W. W. Murdoch, ed., *Environment*, Stamford, Conn.: Sinauer Associates, 1971.

Professor Paul Ehrlich of Stanford University has likened the biosphere to a massive and intricate computer built by linking and cross-linking a vast array of transistors and other electrical components— a mysterious and amazing system that we do not really understand. Man is rapidly simplifying the complex computer network upon which life depends by randomly pulling out transistors, and overloading and disconnecting various parts and circuits. Slowly we are beginning to realize that we are playing a massive game of "ecological Russian roulette," hoping that the computer whose workings we don't comprehend will not break down when we simplify its essential complexity to our purposes. Ecologists don't know how or when our life-support system will break down but they know that if we continue on our present course, sooner or later it will be disrupted.

5–6 Land-Use Planning

But let me end this chapter on a somewhat happier note. All of us use the land and in an industrialized, urbanized society with a rapidly growing population, decisions on how our limited land should be used are everybody's business. In the United States the average population density, that is, the number of people per unit of land, is expected to double in the next 30 to 50 years. As one of our most prominent ecologists, Eugene P. Odum, has pointed out, "the application of ecological principles to land-use planning is now undoubtedly the most important application of environmental science." [6]

Almost all land-use planning has been based on a narrowly conceived engineering approach. Only a few physical variables are analyzed and the side effects — particularly those affecting ecological diversity and the quality of life of the human beings who use the land — are not considered. Really successful urban land-use planning has not been accomplished anywhere; witness the urban blight, sprawl, and increasing social upheaval that characterize almost all of our urban centers.

When we build a highway, shopping center, housing development, or factory the effects, both good and bad, are numerous and

---

[6] Eugene P. Odum, *Fundamentals of Ecology*, 3rd ed., Philadelphia: W. B. Saunders, 1971, p. 420.

usually unpredictable in the long run. As we have already seen our engineering, or straight-line, thinking does not work for a complex cybernetic system. Many short-range benefits (increased jobs and cash flow) have been wiped out by long-range problems (overloaded water supplies, clogged freeways, and increased crime). Most cities in their youthful optimism have said "it can never happen here", but it has happened over and over again. Our cities and landscape are beginning to match poet Kenneth Patchen's vivid description:

"Men have destroyed the roads of wonder, and their cities squat like black toads in the orchards of life."

However, in 1969 a breath of fresh air arrived when Ian L. McHarg, an urban planner, published his book *Design With Nature* [7] — a book that may turn out to be one of the more important publications in this century. It represents a breakthrough in land-use planning and like most important ideas, in retrospect, it seems so obvious and rational you wonder why man has taken so long to discover it.

McHarg shows how we can replace our engineering approach with an ecological, or cybernetic, approach. Basically he suggests that we collect all of the physical data normally used in the engineering approach, namely, geological factors such as soil type and quality, water resources and limitations, and so on. We would then add data based on human value judgments on how the land should be used — historical landmarks, preservation of diversity, wildlife, conservation, and so on. A series of transparent grid maps of the land area are prepared and the data for each variable are plotted on separate transparencies. When these transparencies are superimposed on top of one another, the result is a composite map with varying densities showing how all of the variables combine. A second composite map can be prepared by plotting the distribution of physical disease, crime and social diseases, pollution, ethnic distribution, poverty, income, unemployment, and illiteracy. This health, social, and economic composite — a summary of human problems — can be combined with the first composite to

---

[7] Natural History Press, Garden City, N.Y., 1969.

show suitability of different areas for conservation and urbanization.

If this approach is extended even further by computer simulation and by adding additional ecological variables, it can give all of us a more reliable plan for using our land wisely. This approach has already indicated that we should make certain that at least one-third of our land should be left as national, state, or urban parks, wildlife refuges, green belts, and wilderness areas. Wilderness is disappearing all over the world and in the United States our national park system is greatly overburdened. In our rush to flee our decaying cities and experience the beauty and diversity of natural ecosystems, Americans are literally trampling our parks to death in an embrace of love. Couple this with the more massive damage inflicted by Americans riding through wilderness areas at speeds up to 60 mph on trail bikes and snowmobiles, and we can see why it is urgent that one of our major national goals must be to protect existing natural areas and greatly increase the amount of land under state and federal protection. As an unknown poet once said, "A people without forests is a dying race."

As we newcomers on this planet eliminate threads from the magnificent tapestry of life built up over millions of years of evolution we must remind ourselves that the biosphere is not only more complex than we think, but more complex than we can ever imagine. The essence of survival and freedom requires humility and cooperation rather than arrogance and domination.

What has gone wrong, probably, is that we have failed
to see ourselves as part of a large and indivisible whole.
For too long we have based our lives on a primitive feeling
that man's "God-given" role was to have "dominion
over the fish of the sea and over the fowl of the air and
over every living thing that moveth upon the earth."
We have failed to understand that the earth does not belong
to us, but we to the earth.

Rolf Edberg,
On the Shred of a Cloud

6

World Hunger

6–1 All Flesh is Grass — Food Chains, Pyramids, and Webs

Let us look more closely at what happens to energy as it flows through an ecosystem. In Section 4-3 we listed the major components of an ecosystem and showed how they were related to chemical cycling and energy flow (See Figure 4-4).

A very useful but simplified model pictures people, particularly those in affluent countries, as living at the end of food chains. For example, grass $\longrightarrow$ grasshopper $\longrightarrow$ frog $\longrightarrow$ trout $\longrightarrow$ man.

Energy is transferred from organism to organism in the various levels. A typical food chain might consist of three to four levels, called <u>trophic levels</u>. Plants, or producers, are eaten by herbivores, or primary consumers; small carnivores, or secondary consumers, eat the herbivores; and then top carnivores, or tertiary consumers, eat the small animals.

How much of the initial input of solar energy into plants is actually available to keep animals at the top of the chain alive? Figure 6-1 shows the flow of energy through a typical food chain. The energy input at one end must equal the total energy output in accordance with the First Law of Thermodynamics (See Section 3-2). However, we can see that in accordance with the Second Law of Thermodynamics (See Section 3-3) most of the energy input is degraded to useless heat energy that ends up in the environment. There is a considerable loss of energy at each level, with relatively little actually available to support life. Typically about 80 to 90 percent of the energy is simply wasted and lost as heat to the environment at each step. In other words, only 10 to 20 pecent [1] of the energy stored in the living tissue is available for transfer to the species at the next level.

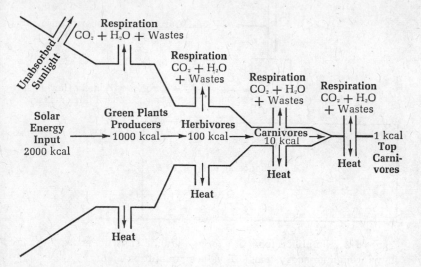

Figure 6–1 Simplified version of energy flow through a food chain. Energy values chosen for illustrative purposes only.

This energy loss at each step can also be expressed in an energy, or food, pyramid, as shown in Figure 6-2.

Another way of looking at this is in terms of the numbers of organisms at each level that are required to support a certain number at the next higher level. This also usually leads to a pyramid, a pyramid of numbers, as shown in Figure 6-3. [2] Six-hundred trout are required to support one man for a year. The trout in turn must

---

[1] Actually the figure varies somewhat with different species and portions of the chain. For example, up to 15 percent of the energy might be transferred from herbivore to carnivore and slightly higher figures might occur in transfer of energy from one carnivore to another. Some organisms have an even lower efficiency of transfer — certain sulfur bacteria have an energy transfer of only 2 percent. Figures 6–1 and 6–2 are designed only to illustrate the basic principle of energy loss in a food chain.

[2] Based on some calculations by Bruce Peterson in the October, 1970 issue of the ZPG Reporter.

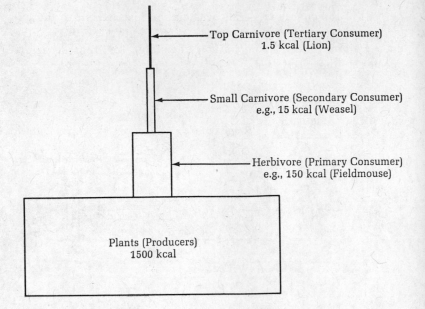

Figure 6–2   Simplified food, or energy, pyramid showing energy flow through an ecosystem. (All values are approximate.)

consume 18,000 frogs, that must consume 54-million grasshoppers, that live off of 2000 tons of grass. Because of the 80-90 percent loss of energy at each level of the pyramid, a small number of large organisms at the top can normally only be supported by a large number of smaller organisms at the lower levels.

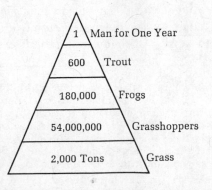

Figure 6–3   Pyramid of numbers in a food chain.

Omnivorous animals, such as man, may eat at all three consumer levels. We are primary consumers when we eat lettuce, secondary consumers when we eat lamb, and tertiary consumers when we eat herring. While it is convenient to talk of linear food chains, as shown in Figure 6-2, such isolated food chains do not actually exist. In nature, many different food chains crosslink and intertwine to form a complex system called a food web. A greatly simplified version of a food web is shown in Figure 6-4.

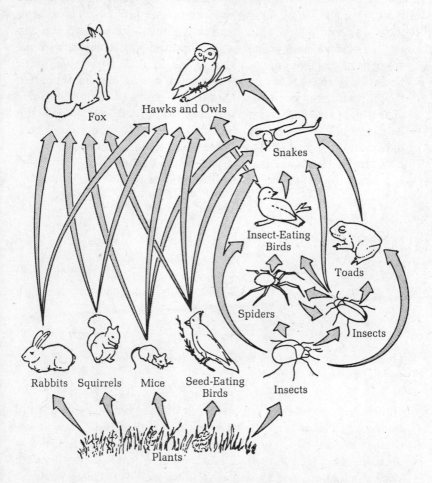

Figure 6–4 Diagram of a greatly simplified food web. (Adapted by permission from William T. Keeton, *Elements of Biological Science,* W. W. Norton & Co., Inc., 1969, 1967.)

6-2 Why Most People in the World Can't Eat Steak — Food Chains and the Second Law of Thermodynamics

The Second Law of Thermodynamics explains the phenomenon that the useful energy available decreases drastically as one goes up a food chain toward man and top carnivores. This degradation of energy as it proceeds through the food chain has far-reaching implications for the overpopulation problem. The shorter the food chain between producer and ultimate consumer, the less the amount of energy lost to the environment as heat, and the greater the relative energy value of the food. For example, going back to Figure 6-3, we can see that more people can be supported by shortening the chain, so that 30 men could be supported for a year if they ate 180,000 frogs instead of trout and 900 people could be supported for a year by consuming about 54 million grasshoppers. Finally, if we could live as low as possible on the food chain by eating 2,000 tons of grass, a population of 2000 people could be supported for a year, as summarized in Figure 6-5.

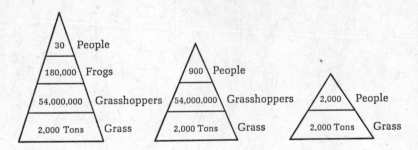

Figure 6-5 By eating further down the food chain a larger population can be supported.

A starving population will be better off, at least in terms of total intake of calories, by eating further down the food chain. It becomes obvious then why most people in the world today must live on a diet of grain rather than meat. Meat will not support a very large population. For example, it takes about 18,000 pounds of alfalfa to support one 2000-pound steer, which might support a 150-pound person for a short time. The second law makes it clear why a pound of steak costs so much more than a pound of corn or wheat. Each year in the United States it takes about 600-million tons of feed to produce only 84-million tons of meat, eggs, and milk. As the human population gets larger and larger, most people have to move to a grain diet based on wheat or rice. The North-American diet is about 25 percent livestock, the European diet 17 percent, and the Asian diet about 3 percent. As the population gets even larger, we may have to move even further down the food chain perhaps eat algae — algae soup, algaeburgers, algae pie, or some form of algae at every meal. (Even this is not practical on a large scale. Algae is fairly indigestible and would require expensive and extensive processing.) We who eat very inefficiently and expensively at the top levels of the food chain forget that most people in the world have very little, if any, meat. We should also realize that our type of diet represents a massive waste and drains off valuable nutrients that could be used to cut down starvation; not to mention the massive pollution that modern agriculture directly and indirectly imposes on the environment.

6–3 World Hunger is Primarily Protein Hunger

Unfortunately, eating only plants (such as algae) in order to get enough calories in a starving world will not work. Most starvation is not caused by a lack of calories but is the result of protein malnutrition and diseases that result directly or indirectly from malnutrition. Unfortunately, plants that contain the most calories generally contain the least protein. A diet based on a plant protein from a single species does not contain all of the amino acids essential for growth and good health.

Thus, world hunger is primarily protein hunger. Since the growth of the brain depends on protein, a lack of protein before the age of three to five years usually means some degree of mental retardation. A recent study in Mexico showed that children who were undernourished before the age of five averaged 13 points lower in I.Q.[3] If this study is correct then from one-third to one-half of the children in the world today are vulnerable to brain damage through protein deficiency.

---

[3] H. F. Eichenwald and P. C. Frye, "Nutrition and Learning," *Science*, *163*, 644-48 (1969).

We who eat at higher levels on the food chain are systematically draining off the protein from our fellow passengers who must attempt to survive on a grain diet. We in the United States drink half of the world's milk and eat three-fourths of its meat. As we add 6,000 more U.S. beef eaters to our population every day, we proclaim a "green revolution" to feed everyone else cereal. We take fish from protein-starved South America and feed it to our livestock, dogs, and cats. Only 17 percent of the annual oceanic fish catch is used as food by poor nations — the remaining 83 percent goes to the developed nations. Each year dogs in the United States consume an amount of protein that would feed 4-million human beings. And this figure is going up; some 10,000 dogs are now born each day in the United States.[4] Professor Georg A. Borgstrom, a distinguished food scientist, has graphically demonstrated the massive protein exploitation of the underdeveloped countries by the developed countries; an exploitation undertaken under the guise of "humane" foreign aid. In 1968, the developed countries shipped approximately 2.5 million tons of *low-grade* grain protein (for example, wheat) to the underdeveloped countries to help them fight protein starvation. During this same year the developed nations took out of the underdeveloped nations about 3.5-million tons of high-grade protein — soybeans, oilseed cakes, and fish meal.[5] This represents a net loss of 1-million tons of protein in underdeveloped countries and an exchange of low-grade for high-grade protein.

It's hard to find heroes and villains in this story. The farmers and fishermen would like to sell their high-grade protein to their own people, but starving and malnourished people have no money. One way of giving aid to developing countries is by purchasing raw materials from them. This enables them to purchase some of the capital equipment they need for their own economic development. As usual, the truth may lie somewhere between gross exploitation and true aid. More likely the problem is that we are not

---

[4] Based on estimates of annual production of meat based dog food.

[5] See G. A. Borgstrom, "The Dual Challenge of Health and Hunger — A Global Crisis," Population Reference Bureau, Selection No. 31, (Jan. 1970), and G. A. Borgstrom, *Too Many*. London: Macmillan, 1969, pp. 32, 323, 325-6.

really paying a just price for the value of these resources. The per capita GNP in the United States has been rising steadily and is now more than $4500 but our per capita cost of raw materials is less than $100, a price no higher than that at the beginning of the century.

6–4 Technological Optimists Keep Forgetting About Thermodynamics

Our circuits are already overloaded with a multitude of "world-shaking" problems, and we want desperately to believe that science or superman or some unknown factor X, will magically and simply solve these complex problems. We are frequently lulled into a false sense of security by glowing reports from technological optimists who fail to understand ecology, thermodynamics, and the mathematical implications of a J-curve. We read in the newspaper about some breakthrough, not realizing the thermodynamic and economic differences between discovering something in the laboratory and carrying it out on a world-wide scale. The first law — the Conservation of Energy — tells us that we can't get something for nothing. A man-made process on a world-wide scale always requires a massive input of energy, money, and time. The second law tells us that whatever we do to order our system, such as growing more food, mining materials, making cars, tractors, planes, plastics, building houses, factories, and cities, producing more fertilizer and pesticides, will always result in a net increase in disorder, or entropy, in our environment. We fail to take this "thermodynamic factor" into account. In addition, man's modern agricultural and technological processes almost always simplify the ecosystem and thus threaten its stability. Finally, because of the J-curve, our impact is no longer local, but global.

The Land Myth

Some suggest that we can grow the food we need by cultivating more land. In advanced countries, such as the United States, the reverse is happening as prime farm land is being taken over for urbanization. In the United States we cover two acres per minute with factories, houses, and stores — over a million acres each year. Highways are now equivalent to paving the entire state of Indiana. We now have one mile of road for every square mile of countryside.[6] In our insatiable need for resources we gouge out 100 to 150 square miles of U.S. land each year as strip mines. At this rate by 2010 we will have defaced by surface mining alone the equivalent of the combined areas of Connectucut, Delaware, Maryland, Massachusetts, and our nation's capital.[7] California produces about 25 percent of the nation's table food, 43 percent of our fresh vegetables, and 42 percent of our nut and fruit crops. Every day California loses 300 acres of agricultural land, and by conservative estimates, at least one-half of California's prime cropland will go to housing and industry by the year 2000; some experts estimate 80 percent. In some places new land can be brought under cultivation, but because it is poorer and has less topsoil, it requires more mechanization, irrigation, fertilization, and pesticides — all taking their toll on the environment. Since 1900 the average depth of topsoil in the United States has decreased from 9 inches to 6 inches. We have been blessed with one of the best pieces of real estate on the planet and in spite of our abuses we have a lot of land left. It is to be hoped we will learn how to use it more wisely.

The Water Myth

Water is the real key to life and to growing food. One-half of the water used in the United States is for agriculture. Our spaceship has a large fixed load of water, but most of it is not *usable* water. Over 97 percent of our water is in the salty oceans. Robert and Leona Rienow[8] have provided a striking example of just how little water on this planet is really usable. Imagine a 12-gallon jug as representing the total water supply on the planet. The entire supply of fresh water would then be about five cups. However, all

---

[6] Lyle, David, "The Human Race Has, Maybe, Thirty-Five Years Left," *Esquire*, September, 1967 and *A Model of Society*, Progress Report of *The Environmental Systems Group*, Univ. of California Institute of Ecology, Davis, Apr., 1969.

[7] Based on figures given in *The Strip Mining of America*, Sierra Club, New York, 1971.

[8] R. Rienow and L. T. Rienow, *Man Against His Environment*, Ballantine Books, Inc., 1970. Highly recommended reading.

but two-thirds of a cup of this are tied up in glaciers. When you remove the additional fresh-water sources deep below the earth's crust, along with that contained in the topsoil and in the atmosphere, and the amount we have polluted, *then the usable water that we have amounts to only about six drops in the bottom of the 12-gallon jug.*

In the past 50 years the per capita use of water in this country has increased twenty-five fold, and our water demands are expected to double by 1980. We think we shall be using 650-billion gallons of water per day by that time. The Senate Water Resources Committee indicates that by 1980 we shall have allocated every last drop of our water from natural sources. You can see why a *usable* water shortage is predicted in the United States by 1980. Please note, we have plenty of water but most of it is not usable.

But can't we desalt the ocean water? Very optimistic estimates by Westinghouse indicate that desalination could supply 1/30 of U.S. water needs by 1984. But we are forgetting the second law. Building and maintaining a vast network of desalination plants would cause a significant entropy increase in our environment, not to mention the resulting mountains of salt that might blow into the sky and affect our weather or be dumped back into the ocean, thus threatening marine life near the coasts. A typical desalting plant might process 1-million gallons per day. To meet our projected needs by the year 2010, we would need 270,000 of these plants along our coastline. Even if the capacity of each plant is somehow increased by a factor of ten, we would still need 27,000 plants. This would take care of all of our shoreline. And to be useful all of this fresh water produced would have to be pumped uphill for hundreds of miles at fantastic expense. We can't get something for nothing.

The Ocean Myth

A great deal of nonsense has been written about the sea as a savior of mankind after we have destroyed the land. Some have the naive idea that the ocean will continue to absorb all the waste we pump into it and at the same time produce all the food we need. There are several reasons why this is another tranquilizing myth. First, it is too expensive in money and energy (don't forget the first law), even if we had the time (don't forget the J-curve).

Second, most of the sea is a biological desert. In terms of food productivity the oceans and deserts tie for last place.[9] An area about as large as the state of California produces about half of the world's fish supply. The major portions of the sea that are rich in plant and animal life are near the coasts. Ninety percent of all saltwater fish are taken in relatively shallow coastal waters. The spawning ground for most of the ocean's life is the estuarine zone where fresh water and salt water mix. The estuaries are probably the richest and most productive life habitats on this planet — habitats we are busily dredging, poisoning, polluting, covering with beach cities, and with nuclear power and desalination plants. Pollution of the world's oceans is one of our most serious crises, and it is projected to increase 700 percent by the year 2000. Making very optimistic projections, probably the best we can hope to do is double or, conceivably, triple the protein from the ocean, which would still provide only about 20 percent of the world's protein.[10]

Third, getting food from the ocean primarily through fish is extremely inefficient from a thermodynamic standpoint, since edible fish are at the top levels of the food chain (See Figure 6-2). It is like trying to feed the world on land by harvesting lions. As a result, the ocean can provide only about 3 percent of the calories for the population of 6 to 7 billion expected by the year 2000.[11] Finally, even if massive harvesting of the sea were feasible, this large-scale tampering with the ocean ecosystem — which we are already doing by dumping in hundreds of thousands of man-made compounds — could result in an ecological catastrophe that could destroy or drastically decrease life in the ocean. Dr. Jacques

---

[9] For a table comparing the productivity of major world ecosystem types, see E. P. Odum, *Fundamentals of Ecology*, 3rd ed., Philadelphia: W. B. Saunders, 1971, p. 52. We dream of rich harvests from the oceans, which are lowest in productivity, while destroying the estuaries with the highest productivity.

[10] National Academy of Sciences, *Resources and Man*, W. H. Freeman & Co., San Francisco, 1969, p. 107.

[11] Even this may be overly optimistic. Many experts claim we are already overharvesting the oceans and recent world fish catches appear to be declining, in spite of new and advanced technology for locating fish. For an authoritative summary of the food potential of the oceans see Chap. 5 in P. Cloud, ed., *Resources and Man — National Academy of Science Report*, W. H. Freeman, 1969.

Cousteau, Dr. Jacques Piccard, and a UN report on marine pollution all warn that at our current rate of pollution there may be little or no life in the ocean by the year 2000.[12] We must use the ocean, but we must use it wisely.

The Synthetic-Food Myth

If the land and the sea will help us but won't save us, then why can't we feed the world with synthetic food, such as the astronauts ate on their trips? Again, this ignores the First and Second Laws of Thermodynamics. Reference to synthetic materials is somewhat misleading. We have never made any new materials, but rather discovered ways of rearranging existing substances in new combinations. To do this on the massive scale needed (the J-curve) would be more expensive in terms of money and energy than trying to grow food on the land (the first law). Furthermore, the resulting air and water pollution and the increase in heat and entropy in the environment from building and maintaining the vast number of chemical plants needed could seriously disrupt the biosphere (the second law). In the distant future laboratory-produced foods will be useful, but they will not solve our problems.

The Education Myth

Can we educate people in the world so that they will recognize and deal with the problem? Optimistically assuming that we could provide the money and teachers, we still have to reckon with the J-curve. We are losing the educational battle. Thirty-five percent of the adults in the world today are illiterate, and although the illiteracy rate is decreasing the number of illiterates is increasing. Each year 7-million illiterates are added; 70 million were added in the last 10 years.[13] Add to this the fact that up to one-half of the

---

[12] See J. Cousteau, "The Oceans Are Dying," *The New York Times*, Nov. 14, 1971 and Schachter, O. and Serwer, D., "Marine Pollution — Potential for Catastrophe," United Nations document OPI/444-06208, April, 1971.

[13] H. Houghton, *Advancement of Science, 115*, 443 (1967) and the UNESCO Survey of Illiteracy cited in *Dateline in Science, 4*, 6 (1969).

children born today — who manage to make it to school age — may suffer brain damage from protein deficiency. These are the people we must reason with in the future. Any progress in education will probably be made by short-circuiting the present formal educational system. This might involve use of transistorized and battery-operated television sets in each world village using a global satellite broadcasting system.

The Evolution Myth

Many ask, "Can't we evolve new lungs or other physiological changes so that we can adapt to a polluted environment?" In addition to blindly accepting the idea that we should go on polluting our atmosphere at an increasing rate, this view rests on a naive view of biological evolution. The time needed for major evolutionary change through a majority of the population's gene pool is measured in hundreds of thousands of years, not in the relatively small number of years imposed by the J-curve. This view also does not recognize that for such changes to occur, billions and billions of people would have to die until the proper mutations occurred in a small number of reproductive individuals. Since it is essentially a random process, it may never occur. The idea that our present problems should be left to the course of biological evolution probably imposes the biggest death sentence of all.

The key lies in social evolution which can take place quickly, rather than biological evolution. We can and must change our way of thinking about our spaceship and our fellow passengers by learning to live in harmony with nature rather than attempting to conquer it.

The Space Myth

I have saved the most naive and absurd myth for last. It is the last stronghold of the "cowboy," or "frontiersman," who, after making a garbage dump out of this spaceship, thinks we can solve our population problem by shipping people off to other planets. With all of our money and technology, we have only managed to make about 12 percent of the surface of this planet habitable; trying to live on most of the so-called wide open spaces that people see from airplanes would result in mass starvation. Let's face it, most countries can't feed their people because they have a poor piece of real estate. But let's wave the biggest technological magic wand of all and do something we can't even do on earth. Let's make all of those unlivable and unappealing planets out there completely habitable. Dr. Garrett Hardin, a prominent biologist, using extremely optimistic assumptions (including an economy-fare ticket), estimates that if we used every dollar earned for one year (our total GNP), we would have enough money to send to nearby habitable planets just *six-days'* increase of the population on this planet (the J-curve again). It would take over 60 times our present GNP each year just to stay even.

We would need to ship away about 70-million passengers a year, or 9000 persons per hour, and of course the exhaust from the millions of spaceships leaving each year would severely damage if not wreck our environment, not to mention the additional entropy and chemical pollution from the industrial plants needed to manufacture these spaceships. Undoubtedly, the people making this trip would have to give up the freedom to have as many children as they want during the trip; thus the really "big breeders" would remain on earth.

The value of our space program relative to the problems here on earth is a hotly debated issue, but the expense involved can probably be justified solely on the fact that it has demonstrated to us all that: (1) we do indeed live on a spaceship — the only real spaceship and (2) we are down to our last planet, and we had better treat it right. The importance of having these fundamental ideas imbedded in the depths of our consciousness cannot be overestimated as a key to dealing with our ecological crisis.

6-5   Growing More Food Is Not Enough

Most experts agree that the only effective way of increasing our food supply is by increasing the yield per acre, as is being done with some of the new high-yield varieties of rice and wheat in what is now called the "green revolution." Unfortunately, these new varieties also require much greater quantities of water, fertilizer, and pesticides, and miracle grains planted as vast monocultures can be wiped out quickly by disease and pests. The "green revolution" also sows the seeds for a social revolution which underdeveloped countries can ill afford — the massive migration of displaced farmers to cities where no jobs await them.[14]

The increased yield in modern agriculture is not based on making more efficient use of solar energy. Instead it is based on supplementing solar energy with massive inputs of fossil-fuel energy to grow more food, as shown in Figure 6-6. The truth is that, in

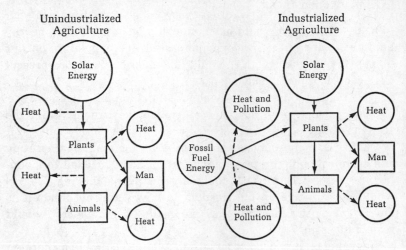

Figure 6–6 Modern agriculture is based on extensive use of fossil fuels.

terms of energy, to grow most of our food requires more energy expenditure than the food itself contains. If fossil fuels and nuclear energy were removed, industrialized countries like the United States would very quickly have an almost total collapse of our specialized, monoculture agriculture. We would have to ask farmers in underdeveloped nations to show us how to survive using unindustrialized agriculture. Of course, our population or at least our level of food consumption would drop sharply. In the

---

[14] For a discussion of the pros and cons of the "green revolution," see L. R. Brown, *Seeds of Change,* New York. Frederick A. Praeger, 1970: N. E. Borlaug, "The Green Revolution: For Bread and Peace, "*Bulletin of Atomic Scientists,* (June, 1971); C. R. Wharton, Jr., "The Green Revolution: Cornucopia or Pandora's Box?" *Foreign Affairs* (April, 1969); and W. C. Paddock, "How Green Is the Green Revolution?" *Bioscience, 20,* 897-902 (1970).

United States we have only about one year's supply of food on hand.

Although growing more food is extremely important in that it buys a little time, this will *not* solve the population problem. It merely treats the symptom, not the disease. As long as the population continues to increase at its present rate, any major gain in food production is only a temporary lull before the food supply is eventually overwhelmed with a tidal wave of new people to feed. To give everyone in the world today the bare minimum diet would require instant doubling of today's world food supply, and still *everyone* would go to bed hungry and malnourished.[15] If everyone in the world today tried to eat at the U.S. level, two-thirds of the people in the world would probably die. Agricultural optimists have for years talked about feeding everyone in the world with this miracle or that, but the truth is they haven't even fed half of those here now, not to mention the additional billions expected in only 30 years. By the year 2000 we will need to triple the world's food supply, an increase in only 30 years greater than has occurred in the 10,000 years since agriculture began (the J-curve again).

Given that we could wave a magic wand and somehow produce enough food, our problem would still not be solved. Having food is one thing, but distributing it evenly to the people throughout the world is another. This requires a sophisticated system of worldwide fertilizer plants, food storage and processing centers, road networks, planes, trucks, railroads, docks, airports, and many other expensive systems. Needless to say, these systems do not exist in most of the world, particularly in the countries that have the largest rates of population growth.

Even more serious, if we could somehow grow and distribute food to the 6- to 7-billion passengers projected by the year 2000, we have to take into account the thermodynamic cost imposed by the second law. Modern agriculture, depending heavily on mechanization, irrigation, fertilizers, chemical control of weeds and pests (herbicides and pesticides), animal-feedlot practices (in which 10,000 to 50,000 animals or up to 250,000 or other poultry

---

[15] Based on the Food and Agricultural Organization of the United Nations (FAO) estimate that from $1/3$ to $1/2$ of the world's population are hungry or malnourished.

are raised in a confined area), and ecosystem simplification. As a result, modern agriculture may represent our most severe and comprehensive disruption of the biosphere.

For example, the use of inorganic nitrogen fertilizer increased 700 percent from 1- million tons in 1950 to 7-million tons in 1969; 50-million tons is the projected need by the year 2000. As we saw earlier, nitrate pollution and two-thirds of our solid wastes in the United States come from agriculture.[16] Fertilizer plants either directly or indirectly add additional pollution to the air and water. The production of 1-million tons of fertilizer requires 1-million tons of steel and about 5-million tons of fuel, mostly fossil fuels.[17]

In the past animal wastes were returned naturally to our soil to aid in the soil-rebuilding process. Modern feedlot, or animal-factory, practices eliminate this natural recycling of nitrogen and produce mountains of animal wastes, most of which overload our water with nitrates. Animal wastes in the United States each year are equivalent to the waste from a human population of 2-billion people. Each year our animal wastes would fill a train reaching from here to the moon and halfway back.

Crop and animal yields can be increased significantly, but many agricultural optimists have forgotten or do not understand the environmental penalty extracted by the second law. As agricultural expert, Lester R. Brown, said: "The central question is no longer 'Can we produce enough food?', but 'What are the environmental consequences of attempting to do so?' "[18]

It is the top of the ninth inning. Man, always a threat at the plate, has been hitting nature hard. It is important to remember, however, that NATURE ALWAYS BATS LAST.

Paul Ehrlich

---

[16] Residents in a California town finally sued a farmer because the mountain of animal wastes on his farm interfered with TV reception.

[17] John McHale, *The Ecological Context*, George Braziller, Inc., New York, 1970, p. 103.

[18] Lester R. Brown, "Human Food Production as a Process in the Biosphere," *Scientific American, 223*, 161, (1970).

7

Pollution, Technology, and Overpopulation

7–1   There Are Two Types of Overpopulation

We now realize that there are two types of overpopulation. The *first type*, which we have in the underdeveloped countries, is overpopulation relative to the food supply. This type already means death for 10- to 20-million human beings each year.

A *second type* of overpopulation is even more serious, because it threatens to disrupt our life-support system. This type occurs in the developed countries, particularly the United States. It is overpopulation relative to consumption of energy and renewable and nonrenewable resources and to the increase in pollution and entropy that automatically results. We might label this second type of overpopulation as <u>overpopullution</u> — too many people consuming too many finite resources and thus polluting the environment. The Western nations plus Japan and Russia account for only about one-quarter of the world's population but use 80 to 90 percent of its natural resources — clear evidence that the developed nations are the greatest threat to the environment.*

Paul Ehrlich [1] and others propose that the level of pollution can be obtained by multiplying three factors: population size, per

---

*Based on figures from the *U.N. Statistical Yearbook, 1970,* United Nations, N.Y.

[1] P. R. Ehrlich and J. P. Holdren, "The People Problem," *Saturday Review,* July 4, 1970, p. 42.

capita consumption, and environmental impact of the consumption (the amount of pollution per unit of production of the particular product).

Overpopullution

$$\begin{matrix} \text{Level of} \\ \text{pollution} \end{matrix} = \begin{matrix} \text{population} \\ \text{size} \end{matrix} \times \begin{matrix} \text{per capita} \\ \text{consumption} \end{matrix} \times \begin{matrix} \text{environmental impact} \\ \text{per unit of} \\ \text{production} \end{matrix}$$

Considerable research is being focused on determining the value of the environmental impact factor for various types of production.[2] As we saw earlier in Table 1-3, the increase in per capita consumption of environmentally harmful products between 1946 and 1968 was on the order of 70 to 2000 percent, while our population increased by about 43 percent.

Actually, the problem is more complex. If we look at a wider range of common products, we find that the per capita consumption of some items increased sharply, some decreased sharply, and some remained about the same, as shown in Table 7-1.

Table 7–1   Changes in consumption and population in the United States between 1946 and 1968*.

Item	Percent Increase Per Capita Consumption
Mercury	2,150
Plastics	1,792
Air freight	593
Nitrogen fertilizer	534
Synthetic organic chemicals	495

(Table continued on next page)

---

*Adapted from B. Commoner, M. Corr, and P. S. Stamler, *Environment*, Vol. 13, No. 3 (1971), 2-19. To get the total increase in consumption multiply each number by 1.43 to allow for the 43% increase in population.

[2] A. J. Van Tassel, ed., *Environmental Side Effects of Rising Industrial Output*, D. C. Heath, 1970; B. Commoner, *The Closing Circle*, Alfred A. Knopf, and footnote to Table 7–1, this page.

Table 7-1 (Continued) Changes in consumption and population in the United States between 1946 and 1968.

Item	Percent Increase Per Capita Consumption
Aluminum	317
Detergents	300
Electric power	276
Pesticides	217
Wood pulp	152
Motor vehicles	110
Motor fuel	100
Cement	74
Truck freight	74
GNP per capita	59
Cheese	58
Poultry	49
Population (% increase)	43
Steel	39
Total freight	28
Total fuel energy	25
Newsprint	19
Meat	19
All fibers	6
Fish	0
Calories	— 4
Protein	— 5
Railroad freight	— 7
Grain	— 22
Lumber	— 23
Cotton fiber	— 33
Wool fiber	— 61
Soap products	— 71

From this table we can see that the basic items for food, clothing, and shelter either decreased or remained at about the same rate as the population increase. The items with a large increase in comparison to population seem to represent the replacement of natural products at the bottom of the list with synthetic ones. See the table below.

New Product replaced	Old Product
Synthetic fibers	Natural fibers (cotton and wool)
Plastics	Lumber
Detergents	Soap
Aluminum & cement	Steel
Truck & airline freight	Railroad freight
Inorganic nitrogen fertilizer	Organic fertilizer
Pesticides	Natural predators
Cars	Railroad and walking

What has happened since 1946 is that we have shifted our production and consumption from less harmful natural products that can be degraded or absorbed in the natural chemical cycles to synthetic products that overload or cannot be absorbed effectively by these ecological cycles. In other words, much of our industrial activity during the past 25 years has been based on introducing counterecological technologies.

In their search for an ecological culprit some have tried to blame technology for the ecological crisis. Hopefully, you can see that it is not technology but our unwise use of some types of technology that is an important factor. To use technology wisely we are going to have to determine the present and projected future impact of each type, along with their social and economic benefits. If the end result is overwhelmingly counterecological we will have to develop counter technologies to control undesirable effects, return to more dependence on natural products (people and clothes were clean when we used soap instead of detergents before 1946), or restrict or not do certain things just because they are technologically feasible.

Unfortunately, some of our more prominent environmentalists [3] have allowed themselves to become trapped into a misleading de-

---

[3] See A. J. Coale, Science, 170, 132 (1970); B. Commoner, M. Corr, and P. J. Stampler, Environment, 13, 2-19 (April, 1971); B. Commoner, The Closing Circle, Alfred A. Knopf, 1971; and the reply by Paul R. Ehrlich and J. P. Holdren, Science, 171, 1212-1217 (1971).

bate over whether population or pollution is the culprit. Hopefully, Forrester's work (see Sections 5-1 and 7-6) should move us beyond oversimplifying a complex cybernetic system with a large number of interconnected variables. This is like arguing over which is more important, your left foot or your right foot or what stops a speeding car, your foot or the brakes? As we saw in section 7-6, both of these variables and others are interconnected in a complex fashion. Consumption of some items has risen faster than population, but obviously all consumption is tied to people in a large number of interconnecting links. In an affluent society the addition of a person amplifies consumption considerably and these two variables together amplify pollution to an even greater extent.

Furthermore we must consider the time it takes to alter these variables. It is possible to decrease or alter consumption patterns very quickly — probably on the order of 5 to 10 years. Unfortunately, as we have seen in Chapter 2, population control through decreasing the birth rate involves a time lag of at least 50 to 70 years. Obviously, we must simultaneously reduce population and consumption patterns, rather than being trapped into dealing with one variable in a multivariable problem.

7–2 The Most Overpolluted Country in the World

In terms of the second type of overpopulation, based on entropy production in the environment, the most overpolluted country in the world is the United States. With only 6 percent of the world's population this nation annually uses about 50 percent [4] of the world's nonrenewable resources and 30 to 40 percent of all the raw materials produced. Extrapolating this consumption rate means that by the year 2000 we will need for our anticipated growth all of the raw materials produced by the noncommunist world.

---

[4] J. L. Fisher and N. Potter, of Resources for the Future, "Resources in the United States and the World," in P. M. Hauser, ed., *The Population Dilemma*. Englewood Cliffs, N. J., Prentice-Hall, 1969, pp. 102, 120-121, 334.

We seem destined to add at least 75-million more Americans by the year 2000—which as President Richard Nixon told us in 1970 is equivalent in terms of people and resources to creating a new city for 250,000 people every 30 days without stop for the next 30 years. This is occurring when we can't even maintain a quality life in our present cities, much less build new ones.

Many people point their fingers at the poor as the culprit. The idea that our population growth results primarily from poor and minority groups (especially black Americans) is a myth based on ignorance and prejudice. The poor produce less than one-third of the babies born each year and less than 20 percent of the babies are nonwhite. According to the Census Bureau the proportion of black Americans in our population is presently 11 percent and it will probably be no higher than 14 percent by the year 2000. Furthermore, affluent blacks, on the average, have fewer children than their white counterparts.

It is dehumanizing and the cruelest of jokes to say that the poor are a major cause of our environmental crisis.[5] They bear the heaviest brunt of the pollution, crowding, and disease, and because their consumption is so small they have relatively little impact on the environment.

It is the rich and middle-class Americans, not the poor, who are threatening our life-support system. We are the megaconsumers and megapolluters, who occupy more space, consume more of each natural resource, disturb the ecology more and pollute directly and indirectly the land, air, and water with ever increasing amounts of thermal, chemical, and radioactive wastes. Professor Wayne H. Davis[6] and others have estimated that the average middle-class American has at least a fifty-fold greater impact on the environment than a typical peasant in a village in India. Assuming that the average poor person in America is three to five times better off than an Indian peasant, this means that *in terms of pollution the typical middle-class American family with three*

---

[5] See W. Ryan, *Blaming the Victim,* New York: Pantheon, 1971 and C. V. Willie, "Perspectives From the Black Community," Population Reference Bureau Selection No. 37, Washington, D.C., June, 1971.

[6] W. H. Davis, "Overpopulated America," *The New Republic,* Jan. 10, 1970.

*children is equivalent to a poor American family with somewhere
between 30 and 50 children.*

The interaction between people and consumption to produce
pollution can also be seen in the Department of Health, Education, and Welfare projections on air pollution from the automobile, as shown in Figure 7-1. The number of Americans is increasing, but the number of cars is increasing twice as rapidly. As a
result, restrictions we have imposed now, if strictly enforced, will
lead to a temporary decrease in air pollution until about 1980;
then air pollution will rise again as the multiplication of the two
factors overtakes the decrease.

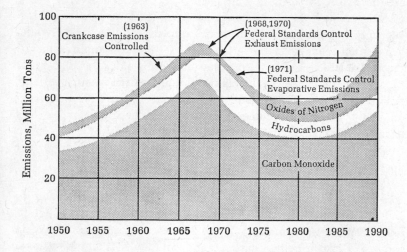

Figure 7-1   Without further restrictions, auto pollution will again
increase. (Source: Department of Health, Education and Welfare.)

One great American myth is that growth always means progress.
This is a useful and perhaps necessary "frontier" rule, when one is
on the lower part of the J-curve. Once around the bend, however,
continued growth cannot mean progress; our continued addiction
to Keynesian economics can only lead to a steady degradation of
life. As Stewart E. Udall put it, "At this moment in history we
need to realize that bigger is not better; slower may be faster; less
may well mean more."

To exist is to pollute and to exist at our level of affluence is to be a super-polluter. Strictly speaking, talk of "cleaning up our environment" and "pollution-free" cars and industries is a scientific absurdity, because of the Law of Conservation of Matter and the First and Second Laws of Thermodynamics. We can decrease pollution but not eliminate it.

In terms of the Law of Conservation of Matter, we never avoid pollution completely — only shift its form and state. Americans are discovering that there is no such thing as a "throwaway" society and no such thing as a consumer. We don't consume anything. We only borrow some of the earth's fixed resources for awhile. We extract them from the earth, transport them to another part of the globe, process them into a new material, and then discard or reuse these materials. Each stage of the process adds some form of pollution to the environment. We can only move pollution from one part of the environment to another, where it may be less harmful. Remember that we are speaking not only of direct harm to man but of harm to the environment and to all of the other species upon which our lives depend.

We can collect dust and soot from the smoke stacks of industrial plants, but this solid must then go into either our water or soil. Cleaning up the "smoke" is misleading. The invisible pollutants left are usually more dangerous and even more expensive to remove. We can collect garbage and solid wastes but they must either be burned (air pollution) or be dumped in our rivers, lakes, and oceans (water pollution) or dumped on the land (soil pollution and water pollution when it washes away). We can expand sewage-treatment plants to deal with water pollution, but if we use present primary treatment methods this can ironically threaten to "kill off" our rivers and lakes by adding even another load of nitrates and phosphates. (See Section 4-6.)

Phosphorus, which is vital for all life, is probably the first chemical that will become unavailable in useful forms,[7] unless we can learn to extract it from the ocean bottom. Yet we "throw it

---

[7] Report issued by the Institute of Ecology, Washington, D.C., Oct., 1971.

away" in detergents, which end up in our rivers and lakes and hasten their oxygen death. This waste is particularly unnecessary, since these detergents are not really necessary to get our clothes clean. [8] The overall result is becoming clear. Lake Erie serves as our early warning system. All lakes eventually die, but it is estimated that we have advanced the death of Lake Erie by probably 150,000 years.[9]

We can reduce air pollution from automobiles by going to electric engines, but this increases air and water pollution by the drastic increase in power plants needed to generate the electricity to recharge the car batteries every night. We can shift to nuclear fission power plants not dependent on fossil fuels, but this increases the thermal pollution of water and the possibility of releasing radioactivity into the environment.

We are slowly coming to the realization that in an ecosystem *we can never do one thing;* that *there is no "away" on a spaceship,* and that ultimately *there is no completely technological solution to pollution,* although technology can help if we use it wisely. Our problem is to choose wisely between the lesser of several evils.

7–4   Are We Running Out of Resources?

While it is obvious that we will eventually run out of nonrenewable resources such as fossil fuels and mineral resources such as iron, lead, uranium, and others, we should realize that our spaceship has the same amount of each element it had millions of years ago, and this amount will not change in the future. Our problem is not one of using resources up but of converting them to less useful or available forms. For example, once a fossil fuel is burned to

---

[8] Withdrawal from "detergent addiction" and clean clothes can be achieved as follows: First strip the detergents from your clothes by washing in hot water to which has been added about 4 tablespoons of washing soda. (Arm & Hammer.) From then on wash a normal load of clothes with one cup of pure soap (e.g. Ivory Snow, flakes or powder) to which has been added 2 to 4 tablespoons of washing soda, depending on the hardness of your water. This may not get your clothes quite as white and bright as the best cleaning detergent but why must we fall for the advertising appeals to get our clothes "whiter than white" — whatever that means?

[9] Charlier, R. H., *New Scientist, 44,* 593-5 (1969).

carbon dioxide or monoxide and water, the solar energy that was stored over millions of years in the form of chemical energy is no longer available. The first law tells us that to take CO_2 and H_2O and to try to convert them back into fossil fuels will take at least the same amount of energy we got out of them. Actually it will take more energy because our energy-producing processes are very inefficient. Furthermore, the second law tells us that all attempts to do this have an unfavorable impact on the environment. In other words these resources, while potentially reusable, are in practice essentially nonrenewable.

What will happen? As we deplete these natural resources, several things may occur. First, the cost of obtaining these resources will rise and as a result some resources may be recycled because the cost of recycling will then become economically feasible. Second, if technologically feasible, we will shift to other sources of energy and materials. For example, one can envision a gradual shift over the next 150 years from fossil fuels to nuclear fission to nuclear fusion to solar, geothermal, and tidal energy — provided, of course, that the technology can be developed and the environmental costs are not too great. The other alternative is a rapid drop in the amount of energy available.[10] In every community for many years to come you and your fellow citizens will be engaged in a continuing debate and battle over our energy crisis. Should we build more nuclear power plants? If so, where? Are there better ways to produce energy? Are we devoting sufficient research funds to develop these sources? And perhaps the most important question — do we really need all the energy we use?

The transformation of energy for human use up to the present has been primarily an engineering and technological problem. It will increasingly become an economic, political, and moral prob-

---

[10] For summaries of our energy crisis see the entire September, 1971 issue of *Scientific American* and the September and October, 1971 issues of the *Bulletin of the Atomic Scientists,* both of which were devoted exclusively to the energy crisis. For a summary of the pro and con arguments for nuclear power see Seaborg, G. T. and Corliss, W. A., *Man and Atom: Building a New World Through Nuclear Technology,* E. P. Dutton, 1971, Chap. 2; Gofman, J. W. and Tamplin, A. R., *Poisoned Power: The Case Against Nuclear Power Plants,* Rodale Press, 1971 and Lapp, R. E., "How Safe Are Nuclear Power Plants?" *The New Republic,* Jan. 23, 1971, p. 19.

lem. *Economic,* because our present energy is obtained primarily by depleting our stocks of nonrenewable resources — coal, oil, gas, and fissionable elements. We are living off of our energy capital, instead of trying to use inexhaustible energy sources — the sun, winds, and tides. *Political,* because with only finite energy resources the problem of which ones are developed and how available supplies are distributed — evenly or unevenly — to people and industries is in the hands of elected officials. *Moral,* because we have to ask whether it is right for some individuals, companies, and countries to consume more than their fair share of nonrenewable resources.

In terms of materials, we might expect a shift from metals to composite materials such as structural plastics, reinforced with glass-fiber and other resin materials. This shift, unfortunately, is in direct conflict with our present rapid depletion of the earth's fossil fuels. They are needed to make plastics and in the long run this is probably their more important use, a factor which we are presently ignoring.

How long will our usable supplies of certain resources last? Nature took about 500-million years to store immense amounts of energy in the form of oil and natural gas, 1-billion years to produce coal deposits, 2-billion years to produce iron and 4-billion years to produce lead deposits. We are depleting the fossil fuels in a span of only several hundred years. In the last 50 years man has used more minerals and fuels than he did in all of his previous history. Whereas early man consumed about 2000 calories per day, the average U.S. citizen now uses directly or indirectly about 200,000 calories daily — a thousandfold increase. The developed nations use about 77 percent of the world's coal, 81 percent of its oil, 95 percent of its natural gas, and about 80 percent of its nuclear energy.[11]

Total energy use in the world is projected to increase by a factor of 5 between 1970 and 2000 and by 800 percent in the United States. The absurdity of such a projection clearly shows the danger of straight-line projections of current trends into the future. In a finite system the J-curve cannot prevail. According to the U.S.

---

[11] Harper, R. A., "The Geography of World Energy Consumption," *Journal of Geography,* Vol. LXV, No. 7, October, 1966, p. 307.

Bureau of Mines the use of coal, oil,[12] and natural gas will increase by a factor of 2 to 4 in the next 30 years, and the use of uranium for nuclear power will increase by a factor of 15. We are caught in an energy dilemma by our insatiable demand for energy, with power needs doubling every 10 years. This and our extremely wasteful use of electricity (at least 30 percent is wasted in the U.S.) are *the real causes of our energy crisis*.

The projected usable [13] supply of some of our important fuels and minerals is given in Table 7-2. Note that these are crude estimates and may be revised up or down as we learn more about the resources actually available.

Table 7–2 Estimated recoverable supplies of certain resources.*

Resource	Years of Exploitable Reserves Left
Aluminum	570
Oil	300?
Coal	250
Iron	250
Natural gas	65
Phosphorus	60
Tin	35
Uranium	30
Copper	29
Zinc	23
Lead	19

*These estimates were obtained primarily from John McHale, *The Ecological Context*, George Braziller, Inc., 1970 (a magnificent book) and G. A. Mills, H. R. Johnson, and H. Perry, "Fuels Management in an Environmental Age," *Environmental Science and Technology, 5*, 30 (1971). For basic studies of resources see references (3), (4), (6), (9), (12) and (13) in the energy and resources section of the bibliography at the end of this book.

[12] Anyone who thinks the great powers will pull completely out of Southeast Asia should be aware that one of the largest untapped sources of oil in the world is there — in South Korea, Taiwan, the Philippines, Malaysia, Burma, Cambodia, North and South Vietnam. Five-billion dollars are to be spent on oil exploration in Southeast Asia in the next twelve years (*Time*, April 12, 1970).

[13] Some can be recovered but only at high economic and environmental costs.

The long-term energy supply, not considering environmental effects, may be favorable. Nuclear fission is being phased in and is expected to supply 40 to 50 percent of our energy by the year 2000. This is severely limited, however, by the supply of uranium, which might last for only about 30 years. Scientists hope to alleviate this problem by the development in the next 10 to 20 years of breeder reactors that regenerate additional nuclear fuel. The real problem with nuclear fission is its environmental impact in the form of thermal water pollution, and the potential danger from the massive amount of radioisotopes that will be produced and have to be transported and stored safely for hundreds of years. Lord Ritchie-Calder[14] estimates that by the year 2000 at any given time there may be over 3,000 six-ton trucks carrying radioactive wastes to "burial grounds." We do not now have a tested method for storing high-level radioactive wastes for long periods of time. The problem of thermal pollution also should not be underestimated. Over 80 percent of all thermal pollution rises from the generation of electricity.[15] By the year 2000, some projected nuclear plants will require cooling water in such large quantities each day that there are only five rivers in the United States with adequate flow to meet these needs. It is estimated that by the year 2000 power plants will need half of all the water runoff in the country for cooling and all of the runoff in summer months.

Most aquatic animal life cannot exist in water above 30 to 35°C. Raising the temperature of water also reduces the solubility of gases, just like heating a soft drink. The amount of oxygen dissolved in water decreases about 17 percent betwen 20 and 30°C. At the same time, the higher temperature increases the metabolic rates of organisms which in turn increase the need for oxygen, and makes the organism more susceptible to some diseases and poisons. In addition, algal blooms from excess nitrate and phosphate are increased with increasing temperature. In other words, excessive thermal pollution can severely disrupt an aquatic ecosystem. On the other hand we might be able to develop systems in which this waste heat is used to grow certain types of fish or other forms of aquatic life that could be used for food. Our problem again is

---

[14] "Mortgaging the Old Homestead," *Foreign Affairs*, January, 1970, p. 211.

[15] Ibid., Mills, Johnson and Perry, p. 31.

one of not really knowing the long-range effects of thermal pollution at a time when our ever-increasing energy demand essentialy stampedes us into committing ourselves to building a vast complex of nuclear power plants.

One hope for the future lies in the development of controlled nuclear fusion as an energy source,[16] as opposed to the more dangerous and environmentally harmful nuclear fission. Nuclear fusion would operate at higher efficiency so that thermal pollution of air and water would be reduced, but of course not eliminated. There is some concern about pollution from tritium released in this process. Unfortunately, at present we are putting most of our money and research effort into developing nuclear fission, rather than fusion. What we really need is an Energy Commission, instead of an Atomic Energy Commission dedicated to promoting the use of only one type of energy.

Another approach, which is also receiving relatively little support, is in improving the efficiency of existing processes so that less of the energy is wasted. Present overall efficiency of energy conversion is about 6 to 10 percent. The internal-combustion engine is about 12 percent efficient and the automobile, with additional energy losses due to friction and other sources, is only about 5 percent efficient, that is, 95 percent of its energy is lost as heat to the environment. A steam-turbine engine on the other hand has an efficiency of about 40 percent and drastically reduces air pollution. Fuel cells potentially have an efficiency up to 80 percent.

The "cleaner" sources of energy which we have not been able to tap effectively are geothermal (tapping into the heat inside the earth), tidal, and direct use of solar energy. Solar energy is the cleanest because the primary entropy increase occurs in the sun — a gigantic nuclear fusion reactor some 93-million miles away. In reality, it is the only source of energy that allows us to escape most of the consequences of "entropy trap" on our spaceship. Unfortunately, all of these possibilities are a long way off, if they are ever developed, and cannot be expected to help us significantly in our present short-range transition period.

---

[16] For a summary of the prospects for nuclear fusion see Gough, W. C. and Eastlund, B.J. "The Prospects of Fusion Power," *Scientific American*, Feb. 1971, pp. 50-64 and Rose, D.J., "Controlled Nuclear Fusion: Status and Outlook," *Science*, May 21, 1971, pp. 797-808.

In summary, *the limitation of energy consumption in the next 30 to 100 years does not seem to lie in any critical shortage of resources but in the impact on the environment from using these resources,* as shown in Figure 7-2 and earlier in Figure 7-1.

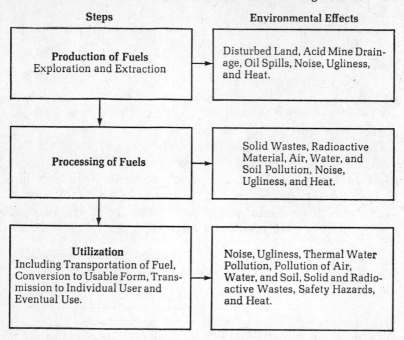

Steps	Environmental Effects
Production of Fuels Exploration and Extraction	Disturbed Land, Acid Mine Drainage, Oil Spills, Noise, Ugliness, and Heat.
Processing of Fuels	Solid Wastes, Radioactive Material, Air, Water, and Soil Pollution, Noise, Ugliness, and Heat.
Utilization Including Transportation of Fuel, Conversion to Usable Form, Transmission to Individual User and Eventual Use.	Noise, Ugliness, Thermal Water Pollution, Pollution of Air, Water, and Soil, Solid and Radioactive Wastes, Safety Hazards, and Heat.

Figure 7–2 Pollution and the use of power.

Since all of our energy conversion processes result in adding heat to the environment, the ultimate pollutant is heat. When man's activities generate more heat than the atmosphere can radiate back into space, the atmosphere will begin to heat up. If our present energy use continues to increase about 7 percent per year, then the critical 3°C rise in temperature of our atmosphere could occur somewhere in the next 100 to 165 years.[17]

We are thus led to consider two fundamental questions. What

---

[17] For detailed discussions of heat limits see A. B. Cambel, "Impact of Energy Demands," *Physics Today,* December, 1970, p. 41; S. F. Singer, "Human Energy Production as a Process in the Biosphere," *Scientific American, 223,* 174 (1970); and J. Harte and R. H. Socolow *Patient Earth,* New York, Holt, Rinehart and Winston, 1971, Chapter 17.

level of population should we have on our spaceship and what patterns of energy and resource consumption should we develop so that all — not just some of the optimum number of passengers — can lead quality lives with freedom and dignity?

Professor J. A. Campbell [18] and others have made estimates of the world population that could be supported at present U.S. levels of consumption by existing resources, as summarized in Table 7-3. It must be emphasized that these are crude estimates.

These estimates assume that we adopt entirely new or much improved methods for using resources and that the rate of use does not increase over our *present* U.S. levels and that these methods do not wreck or disrupt our environment. They are probably somewhat deceiving, because they represent maximum levels. For example, the projection for 30-billion people in terms of food is based on the estimated total photosynthetic capability of plant life on the planet. It assumes that (1) everyone in the world is on a vegetarian diet — no meat would be available for anyone because it is wasteful of food energy; (2) there is no other animal life or

Table 7-3 Maximum World Population Potentially Capable of Being Supported at Present U.S. Levels of Consumption of Existing Resources.

Present World Population = 3.5 billion
Projected World Population by 2030 = 10 billion

Resource	Population (in billions)
Maintaining or increasing the overall quality of life	.5–2
Preserving the quality of our life support system	1–5
*Heat buildup	10
Food	30
Oxygen	100
*Space	100
*Energy	100
*Water	100

*See J. A. Campbell, *Chemical Systems*, W. H. Freeman & Co., 1970.

[18] *Chemical Systems*, W. H. Freeman & Co., 1970.

insect life to compete with man for the plants; and (3) that we would consume the entire plant, leaf, stalk, and so forth.

In terms of maintaining the quality of life and the quality of our life-support system, we have probably already greatly exceeded the maximum population figure.[19]

7-5 The First and Second Thermodynamic Revolutions

The developed countries have engineered what might be termed the *first thermodynamic revolution*. It consists of a dramatic increase in material goods, broad political participation, and education for a high percentage of their citizens. It has been based, however, on improving the system at the expense of the surroundings and the thermodynamic debt required by the second law is now coming due.

Two-thirds of the world's population have yet to participate in this first thermodynamic revolution. People talk glibly about underdeveloped countries becoming developed by following the American approach to industrialization. What would happen if the present level of American industrialization was extended throughout the world? Within a short time the planet would be uninhabitable. To provide automobiles at the U.S. level of one to every three persons would require 2300-million tons of steel when the world production is only 500-million tons. Our atmosphere would contain about 200 times more sulfur dioxide and 750 times more carbon monoxide and carbon dioxide. Our lakes, rivers, and oceans would be loaded with 175 times more chemical wastes, and thermal pollution could completely disrupt our aquatic ecosystems. Two-thirds of the world's forests would be eliminated, and each year 30-million acres of farmland would be converted to cities and highways.[20]

The only hope of the underdeveloped countries and our only hope for preserving and increasing the quality of life lies in our

---

[19] Scientists continue to debate what the maximum and optimum populations might be while millions die. It is somewhat analogous to passengers in a speeding car on a crowded street debating whether 80, 90, or 100 miles per hour is an unsafe speed.

[20] Cousins, N., *Saturday Review*, June 20, 1971, p. 18.

ability to bring about a *second thermodynamic revolution*. It would be an ecological revolution that involves taking the Second Law of Thermodynamics seriously. It would mean that our agriculturists, engineers, doctors, and indeed all of us take into account the impact of any of our actions on the surroundings — not just for the present but also for future generations who will inherit this still beautiful planet.

At the same time that the first thermodynamic revolution threatens the survival of our life-support system, the second thermodynamic revolution has provided us with the concept of cybernetics, a revolution in the use and handling of information. If wisely used, it can allow us to analyze complex systems and anticipate problems and solutions rather than responding only to crises. Let us look more closely at this approach.

7-6 World Models — Intuitively Obvious Solutions May Lead to Disaster

In Chapter 5 (See Section 5-1) we saw that we apparently cannot make valid projections on what will happen in complex cybernetic systems. Indeed, our intuitive conclusions often turn out to be the opposite of the real situation. Our short-range and sincere attempts to improve a situation often in the long run only make matters worse.

We described the exciting and important work being done by Professor Jay Forrester and Professor Dennis Meadows of MIT in computer simulation of cybernetic models of the world ecosystem. They looked at the interaction of six major variables — population, pollution, natural resources, capital investment, food production, and quality of life. Let us now look more closely at their approach and see some of their conclusions.

Since any model or theory is no better than the basic assumptions upon which it is built, let's begin with them. They seem straightforward and reasonable:

1. The birth rate is increased by greater food production and decreased by crowding, pollution, and a high standard of living.

2. The death rate is increased by pollution and crowding and

decreased by increased food production and a high standard of living.

3. Increased capital investment increases pollution, standard of living, and nonrenewable resource depletion. Initially it increases food production but the increased pollution eventually leans to decreasing food production.

4. Increased capital investment leads to a rise in the standard of living.

5. Quality of life is increased by increasing food and standard of living and is decreased by pollution and overcrowding.

These basic assumptions and the more detailed interconnections shown earlier in Figure 5-3 were simulated by the computer for the 200-year period from 1900 to 2100. Known facts about the period from 1900 to 1970 were used to test the validity of the model. A particular variable is chosen and its impact on the other variables is simulated and the projected future changes in each variable are plotted out by the computer.

Let us ask some questions and look at the simulated answers.

Question No. 1: What might be the effect of reducing the rate of depletion of our nonrenewable resources by 25 percent, beginning in 1971?

Answer: Although intuitively we expect a reduction in the rate of resource use to decrease pollution, Figure 7-3 shows that such a decrease could lead to a rise in pollution around 2050 that is 40 times higher than that in 1970. As a result, the world population which has reached about 5.8 billion by 2030 crashes to less than 1 billion between 2030 to 2070. Note that we are reducing the rate of resource depletion. This means that the plot of natural resources still goes down, but not as steeply after 1971.

Question No. 2: What might be the effect of increasing capital investment by 25 percent, beginning in 1971?

Answer: Here our intuitive ideas may be closer to the simulated projections — at least if you have joined the group of people who realize that ever-increasing GNP and industrialization may not be the sweet sound of progress but the gloomy sound of our funeral

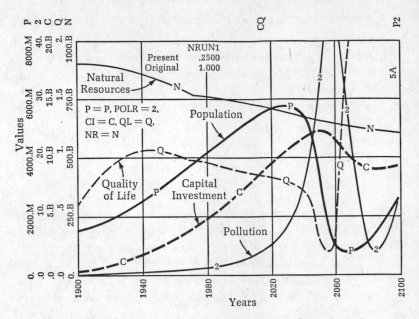

Figure 7–3 A 25% reduction in usage rate of natural resources in 1971 leads to a pollution crisis and a population crash.[21]

march. Figure 7-4 shows that a 25 percent increase in investment in 1971 could cause a short run rise in the quality of life between 1971 and 1985 — but after that it falls sharply. The resulting increased industrialization of the planet could lead to a twenty-fold increase in pollution around 2030. Population increases to about 5.5 billion by 2010 and then crashes to about 1 billion by 2050.

Question No. 3: What might be the effect of reducing the world birth rate by 30 percent, beginning in 1971?

Answer: Figure 7-5 shows that this helps temporarily but after a brief pause population still increases to about 4.5 billion around 2020 and then declines slowly to about 3 billion by 2100 because of natural resource depletion.

Question No. 4: The curves in Figure 7-5 were better but still not encouraging because of natural-resource depletion. So let's

---

[21] Figures 7–3 through 7–9 are reproduced with permission from J. W. Forrester, *World Dynamics*, Cambridge, Mass.: *Wright-Allen*, 1971.

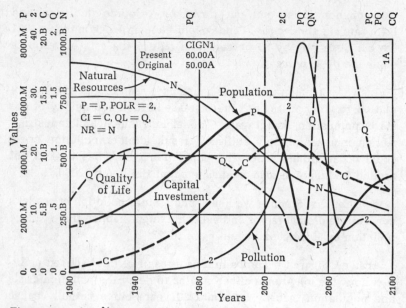

Figure 7–4   A 25% increase in capital-investment in 1971 triggers a pollution crisis and a population dieback.

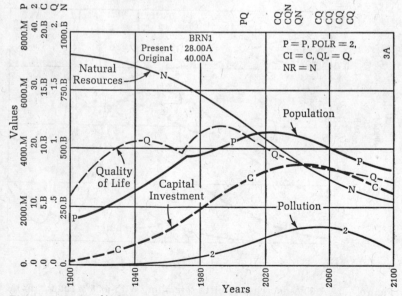

Figure 7–5   A 30% decrease in birth rate in 1971 still leads to population growth followed by a decline as natural resources are depleted.

use common sense and cut down on resource depletion and birth rate simultaneously. What might happen if beginning in 1971 we cut birth rate by 30 percent and reduce the rate of resource depletion by 25 percent?

Answer: Common sense fails again, as is seen in Figure 7-6. Population growth pauses until the increase in food and quality of life starts population rising again. Capital investment and industrialization increase sharply and as a result another pollution crisis could occur around 2050. The population which has peaked out around 5.8 billion in 2030 crashes to about 1 billion by 2060.

Question No. 5: Since we keep running into pollution crises let's concentrate on that factor and ask what might happen if we reduce pollution by 30 percent, beginning in 1971?

Answer: Figure 7-7 shows that as a result of this reduced pollution now, the long-range effect may be to delay the pollution crisis and population dieback by about 20 years but eventually cause

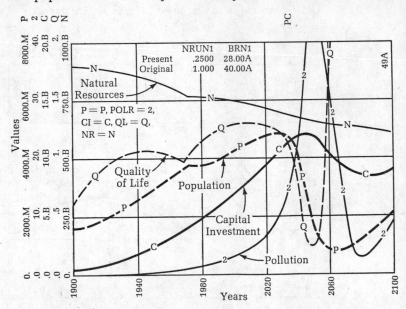

Figure 7–6   A 30% decrease in birth rate along with a 25% reduction in resource usage rate still leads to a pollution crisis and population dieback.

even more people to die. The population increases to about 6.5 billion by 2030 and then crashes to about 1.5 billion by 2090.

Question No. 6: Let's get serious and do several things simultaneously. What might happen if we reduce pollution by 30 percent, reduce resource rate usage by 25 percent, and increase food production by 25 percent, all beginning in 1971?

Answer: It would seem wise to increase food production as we are already striving to do, but this causes the population to rise even faster than in Figure 7-7 and triggers off the pollution crisis and an even greater population dieback 20 years earlier, as shown in Figure 7-8. Between 2040 and 2080 the population drops from about 7 to 1.5 billion.

Question No. 7: What is the best way out of this mess?

Answer: Professor Forrester and his colleagues found that the transition to a new world equilibrium state (J- to an S-curve) that would give a high quality of life without a major population die-

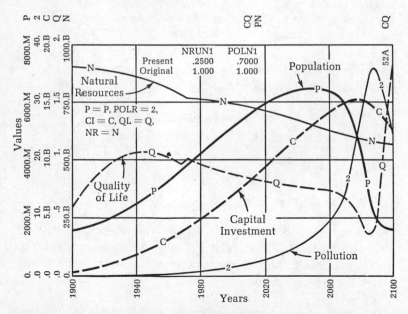

Figure 7–7   Reduction of pollution generation by 30% only delays the pollution crisis and population crash by about 20 years.

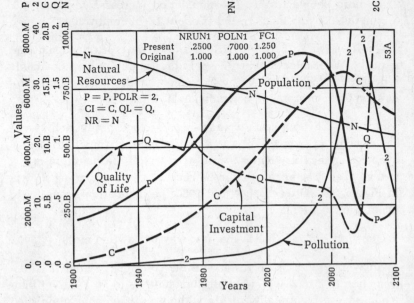

Figure 7–8 Reducing pollution by 30%, resource rate usage by 25% and increasing food production by 25% causes an earlier and even greater pollution crisis and population crash.

back would require the following immediate changes in what we are doing:

1. A 75 percent reduction in natural-resource usage rate.

2. A 50 percent reduction in the pollution generation rate.

3. A 30 percent reduction in the birth rate.

4. A 40 percent reduction in capital-investment generation.

5. A 20 percent reduction in food production.

The projected results of instituting these changes now are shown in Figure 7-9. The result is a slight drop in population and by 1985 a stabilization of the quality of life at a value slightly higher than we had in 1970.

Our first common sense reaction to such a projection is probably, "How absurd can you get?" These changes run directly counter to our entire political-economic system and to the rising

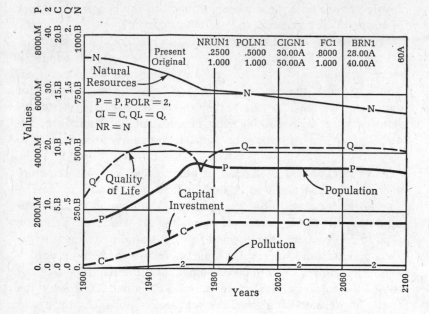

Figure 7–9   Reducing resource rate usage by 75%, pollution by 50%, birthrate by 30%, capital investment by 40% and food production by 20% leads to the most stable transition.

demands for food, housing, jobs, medical care, and industrial development. Immediate institution of these changes would undoubtedly increase the death rate because of the resulting catastrophic depression. We are damned if we do and damned if we don't.

Is there a way out of the dilemma? With worldwide action, led primarily by the United States, over the next 30 to 50 years we could achieve a transition not so smooth as that in Figure 7-9 (with good long-range effects and bad short-range effects) but not so catastrophic as those predicted in earlier figures.

As Forrester points out, the model is still crude and greatly oversimplified.[22] But he contends that it is still better than the mental models we now use for national and global planning. We must always use some type of model — the question is whether we can

<hr />

[22] See D. H. Meadows, D. L. Meadows, et al., *The Limits to Growth,* New York: Universe Books, 1972, for an improved model of this work. The results and conclusions are basically the same.

develop better ones more closely attuned to the cybernetic nature of our political, economic, and ecological systems.

Many other factors need to be added to the model. For example, it does not take into account the possibility of developing a steady-state economy [23] with all key resources being recycled. Probably one of the most important problems existing today is for our best economists to devote themselves to developing a steady-state economy and working with our best political minds to develop a plan for instituting this crucial change over the next 20 to 30 years.

The model should be refined in other ways. The age structure of the population needs to be included, renewable and nonrenewable resources need to be separated, and the possibility of substitution needs to be included; the different kinds of pollution need to be examined, the effects of using capital investment to reduce pollution and to recycle resources instead of being used primarily for growth need to be examined, and the nature and diversity of the world political systems could be added. Obviously, the model at present is too simplistic and leaves out many important variables. Although we should not take the specific predictions of his model literally, it may still be a better predictor than our present intuitive models.

We can perhaps draw some tentative conclusions from this important study.

1. The problem is a complex cybernetic mix of a number of factors and we *must* deal with all of them simultaneously. Focusing on only one variable such as population, pollution, or industrialization will not work.

2. Although all variables must be dealt with simultaneously, industrialization may be the most disturbing force in the world ecosystem. As a result a society with a high level of industrialization may not be sustainable. It may be self-extinguish-

---

[23] For a discussion of this crucial idea see J. J. Spengler, "Economic Growth in a Stationary Population," Population Reference Bureau Selection No 38, Washington, D.C., July, 1971; H. E. Daly, "Toward a Stationary State Economy," in J. R. Harte and R. H. Sorolow, *Patient Earth.* New York: Holt, Rinehart and Winston, 1971; and J. A. Wagar, "Growth verses the Quality of Life," *Science, 168* 1179-1184 (1970), and footnotes 14 and 15, Chapter 9.

ing as it exhausts the finite resources upon which it depends. This results primarily from the fact that our population-pollution crisis is an entropy crisis — we can't repeal or ignore the Second Law of Thermodynamics.

3. There may be no realistic hope for the present underdeveloped nations to become industrialized.

4. While there are ways to soften the transition from a J- to an S-curve, we may now be living in a "golden age." In spite of our feeling that something is wrong, the quality of life may be, on the average, higher than ever before in history and higher than it will be in the future.

5. That "common-sense," or "intuitive," thinking and projections may fail because as Forrester points out they lead to several traps:
   — the attempt to relieve one problem is likely to produce unpredictable and even more unpleasant problems;
   — short-term improvement often leads to much greater long-term degradation;
   — the local parts of a system often conflict with the goals of the larger system;
   — intuition often leads people to intervene in a system at points where little leverage exists.

6. That in our finite system exponential growth of population and industrialization will eventually cease, regardless of what we do. But if we understand our predicament and take appropriate action, we can avert catastrophe.

7. Finally, and most important, computer simulation and other devices may be crucial in helping us understand complex systems, but in the final analysis our entire dilemma comes down to a *human problem of values*. How much do we really care about future generations — even our own children who will inherit what's left of our ecosystem? Do we really care about preserving our life-support system? Do we really care about our fellow passengers?

These are the real questions and we must face them now as we never have before. To avoid this is to deny the essence of our humanity.

A check list from Genesis I, 28.[24]

☒ Be fruitful, and multiply

☐ and replenish the earth,

☒ and subdue it!

☒ and have dominion over the fish of the sea,

☒ and over the fowl of the air,

☒ and over every living thing that moveth upon the earth.

[24] Adapted from an ad appearing in *Time* magazine by the Barbetta-Miller Advertising, Inc., Bill Gentry, copywriter, and Ed Szep, art director.

8

A Case for Hope

8–1 Have We Booked Passage on the Titanic?

Psychologist Rollo May says that many of us are losing our ability to care about anyone or anything because we feel overwhelmed. We have a feeling of powerlessness — our lives seem to be managed by impersonal and uncontrollable forces. We feel alienated, polarized, fragmented, and isolated from nature and from other human beings as a result of a society emphasizing specialization, that is, an atomization and encapsulating of the human spirit — our most vital resource.[1] More are finding the goals we seek are, in fact, without meaning. We feel we don't know where we are going or where we should go.[2] Couple this confusion and uncertainty with the fact that a large portion of our finest minds, energies, and resources are being absorbed by killing and devastating. Add to this our immense power to destroy ourselves by nuclear or ecological holocaust and it is not surprising that many wonder if there really is any hope. Have we booked passage on the Titanic?

---

[1] See Robert G. Franke, "The Biologist, the Psychologist, and the Environmental Crisis," *Bioscience, 21,* 221 (1971).

[2] One is reminded of the airline passengers who heard the following announcement over the loudspeaker. "This is your captain. I have both good and bad news. The good news is that we are making rapid progress at 600 mph. The bad news is that I don't know where we are or where we are headed. This is a recording."

Should we all become swinging hedonists and have one "helluva" party while the ship inevitably goes down?

The most important message of this book is that the answer to these questions is a resounding NO — probably the most important NO in the history of mankind. Teilhard de Chardin once said, "It is too easy to find excuses for inaction by pleading the decadence of civilization or even the imminent end of the world." There are probably three human forces that can kill us: (1) *blind technological optimism,* following those who say, "Don't worry, science or some fairy godmother will save us;" (2) *gloom-and-doom pessimism,* giving up because of those who say there is no hope; and (3) *our own greed, apathy, and refusal to face reality,* giving up concern and involvement through an easy but fatal fatalism or acting on the basis of a naive view of reality.[3]

What is the case for hope? It does not, of course, rest on provable facts or rational analysis. John W. Gardner, former Secretary of Health, Education, and Welfare, and now chairman of Common Cause, the people's lobby, has eloquently stated why hope is one of the greatest driving forces in life — a force that transcends optimism and pessimism.

"No doubt the world is, among other things, a vale of tears. It is full of absurdities that cannot be explained, evils that cannot be countenanced, injustices that cannot be excused. Our conscious processes — the part of us that is saturated with words and ideas — may arrive at exceedingly gloomy appraisals, but an older, more deeply rooted, biologically and spiritually stubborn part of us continues to say yes to hoping, yes to striving, yes to life. All effective action is fueled by hope."[4]

In a fast-changing, exceedingly complex world we have apparently lost our confidence. Paradoxically, it was our overconfidence

---

[3] McLandburgh Wilson said, "The optimist sees the doughnut, but the pessimist sees the hole." Perhaps we should add that the naive realist sees the doughnut and the hole but the ecological realist tries to see the doughnut and the hole and their relationship to the biosphere.

[4] John W. Gardner, *The Recovery of Confidence,* W. W. Norton & Company, Inc., New York, 1970.

that the world was essentially infinite and that we had dominion over it, that led us to the present ecological crisis. Hope lies in our ability to rekindle a more realistic confidence — a new confidence based on a revolution in human consciousness that truly accepts our limitations. It means accepting and acting on the basis that we live in a finite world. The purpose of the previous chapter was not to overwhelm you with gloom and doom, but to overwhelm you with the fact that we do indeed live on the only real spaceship — there is no escape from this fact. Because of this and the First and Second Laws of Thermodynamics, there can be no technological advance without the social or environmental cost of resource consumption and waste accumulation, however delayed the presentation of the final bill may be.

My purpose has been not to show you what the future will necessarily be, but to show you where we appear to be heading, if present trends continue. As René Dubos reminds us, "trend is not destiny."[5] George Orwell's famous book 1984 was designed to aid us in preventing one kind of possible future. The history of mankind demonstrates the capacity of man to change radically his world view and to act quickly and often unexpectedly on the basis of a new consciousness. Biological evolution takes millions of years, but cultural change can occur rapidly, even more rapidly today because of the speed and potential power of mass communication. Possible futures based on extrapolation of present trends will probably occur only if we give up in despair and assume they are inevitable.

8-2 The Future Depends On the Things We Give Up

Accepting and adopting a spaceship consciousness means not only that we can no longer have or do everything we want, but that we cannot afford the notion that we think we can. This dangerous dream must be replaced with an ecological dream of man living in harmony with nature and his fellow man in a closed but not a static system. A balanced ecosystem is based on exciting diversity and complexity in a maze of continuous change — but

---

[5] René Dubos, "The Despairing Optimist," The American Scholar, 40, 16-20 (Winter, 1970-71).

change within the limits imposed by the system. Achieving this dynamic steady-state dream instead of the false drive of over-simplification of nature and ever-accelerating change and growth is not only possible but necessary. It means we must make choices; we can only have more of this if there is less of something else.[6] We can only increase the quality of life by limiting the number of passengers and their energy-consuming activities. J. Irwin Miller,[7] Chairman of the Board of Cummins Engine Company has expressed the reality which we as Americans must face.

> "The real price of the future is our willingness to grow up and become an adult people — to make choices rather than to avoid them. When we ask what our national priorities should be and how we should allocate our national resources, we are posing questions we have never in our history supposed we would have to ask. We never thought Americans would have to choose. For the first time we are beginning to realize that we can't have everything. The price of the future, then, will be found in the things we give up *in order to gain the things that are compatible with the limitations of living on a spaceship.*"

Charles Reich,[8] in his useful but controversial book, *The Greening of America,* indicates that our refusal to face reality is the true source of powerlessness and he also calls for a revolution in consciousness. He categorizes Americans as existing in three levels of consciousness. Consciousness I is the traditional outlook of the farmer, small businessman, and worker. It is based on a simple but decent life with reverence for morality, hard work, self-denial, patriotism, and limitations on big government, big business, and the rate of change. Reich indicates that this represents a dream world that no longer exists in our industrialized state based on big business and government. Consciousness II is the modern outlook of an organizational society based on planning,

---

[6] It is not quite as bad as Ralph Lewin indicated when he said, "Everything I like is either illegal or immoral, pollutes the environment or increases the population."

[7] J. Irwin Miller, "Changing Priorities: Hard Choices, New Price Tags," *Saturday Review,* January 23, 1971, p 36. Emphasis added.

[8] Charles A. Reich, *The Greening of America,* New York: Random House, Inc., 1970.

liberal reform, and continued growth and change through technology. Consciousness III, which Reich advocates in place of I and II, is a new humanism that rejects or is suspicious of logic, rationality, analysis, thought, and organization and replaces it with being true to oneself, respect for the absolute worth of every human being, a sense of spontaneity, community, honesty, peace, sharing, and caring. He envisions this revolution occurring merely by allowing it to sweep spontaneously through the minds of our youth and citizens.

Unfortunately, Reich's vision, while appealing and superb as far as it goes, is not large enough. It too founders on unreality. It does not take into account our finiteness or the Second Law of Thermodynamics which always requires continual organization and action for survival and a quality life, or the J-curve which does not provide us with the luxury of waiting around for something to happen to us. His view is also narrow in that it does not recognize that the true strength and hope for America and the world is found by preserving the essential diversity found in all three levels of consciousness, along with many other qualities his oversimplified classification omits. The resistance to change found in Consciousess I, the organizational skills in Consciousness II, and the sensitivity to human dignity in Consciousness III are all essential ingredients in a steady-state world. They and other elements must be combined and used in a synergistic pluralism — a new consciousness based on a blend of the new humanism with an ecological understanding of the need for diversity, stability, and organization in a steady-state system.

8–3 All the News Isn't Bad — The People Are Stirring

There are grounds for cautious hope that such a value revolution is underway in this country. People are stirring, questioning, listening, and organizing. In spite of all the noise and confusion, and the gap between rhetoric and reality (the R and R gap), more and more Americans are beginning to question our institutions and purposes. They are asking, "What is true wealth? What have we done wrong? What should be the true aims of our affluent nation?" It is particularly significant that some of our youth are educating their elders by making them take a fresh look at these crucial questions.

Some politicians are beginning to listen and act and to stop treating the average voter as a naive child who wants to be told that there are simple solutions, that we are not really in trouble, and that more and more progress based on a blind use of technology will lead to the promised land. There is a new awareness that the key to leadership lies in telling people the truth — that we can't have everything, that we are in deep trouble, that we must make some significant and difficult changes, that for everything we want to preserve we will have to give up something, that the heaping of crisis upon crisis need not be taken as a forecast of doom but the birthpangs of a new world where we finally face up to the questions of what is man and what is his place in the world.

As Patrick Moynihan, former counselor on urban affairs to the President of the United States, said: "... the essence of tyranny is the denial of complexity. What we need are great complexifiers — men who will not only seem to understand what it is they are about but who will also dare to share that understanding with those for whom they act." The American public recognizes that as H. L. Mencken put it: "for every problem there is a solution — simple, neat, and wrong." When more of our leaders recognize this they will be able to mobilize our vast reservoir of human energy, creativity, and conscience in a massive *spaceship-earth program.*

Professor J. M. Stycos of Cornell University has observed that major social changes go through four stages:

Evolution of Social Change

Phase 1: No Talk — No Do
Phase 2: Talk — No Do
Phase 3: Talk — Do
Phase 4: No Talk — Do

It seems incredible that in only a three-year period between 1966 and 1969 the majority of U.S. citizens became aware of and concerned about our environment. In terms of pollution we have already moved partially into Phase 3 in only five years time. In terms of population we have moved into Phase 2 and made some timid movements into Phase 3.

During the past five years environmentalists have become much better organized and informed. More important, they have learned how to use legal and political machinery as well as, and in some cases better than, their corporate opponents. There are a few signs that some industrialists may be shifting from their earlier positions of defensiveness and lack of ecological understanding. Some are beginning to see that the public is serious, that in the long run pollution is bad for business, that the longer they wait the greater the costs of cleaning up, and that cleaning up the environment is a major market in itself.

Slowly citizens' groups are forming to protect the environment, to challenge the priorities and assumptions of elected leaders, to insist on equal rights for all Americans — male or female, black, red, brown, or white — to protect the consumer, to lobby for the common man as a counterbalance for the powerful lobbies of organized business and other interests, to use existing laws in a creative way to protect the poor, the disadvantaged, and indeed all of us. In the past few years we have seen the development of a powerful ecological lobby led by David Brower, director of Friends of the Earth, the rise of public-service lawyers, inspired and led by Ralph Nader, the formation and merger of consumer-protection groups, and the formation of a people's lobby, Common Cause, led by John W. Gardner. While many sit on the sideline talking about how the system can't be changed, these groups *are* changing the system.

These are not mass movements as yet, but they are growing. Political analysts indicate that it probably requires dedicated political activity by only about 10 percent (perhaps less) [9] of the population to bring about significant change. In the 1970 elections a number of the candidates with the worst environmental records were defeated.

I am not suggesting that everything is going well; rosy and naive optimism is not in order. We have only begun to recognize our predicament — much less decide on courses of action. Some cyn-

---

[9] Some estimate only 5 percent or less, but it probably takes an additional 5 percent to counteract the 5 percent who will organize against almost any movement.

ics say that ecology is a fad. If it is, it will be the last fad. There will be much confusion and disagreement and many will hop off of the ecology bandwagon once they realize the really fundamental changes it requires. But there is considerable room for hope.

The ecological, or second thermodynamic, revolution will be the most all-encompassing revolution in the history of mankind. It involves questioning and altering almost all of our ethical, political, economic, sociological, psychological, and technological rules or systems. No one could ask for a more challenging and meaningful way in which to devote his life. It will not involve dramatic breakthroughs, but only day-to-day hard work, many setbacks, extremely bitter disputes, frustration, anguish, and the joy that comes from caring for the earth and our fellow passengers. It is an exciting time to be alive!

Human default or degradation can reach a point where even the most stirring visions lose their regenerating or radiating power. This point, some will say, has already been reached. Not true. It will be reached only when men are no longer capable of calling out to one another, when the words in their poetry break up before their eyes, when their faces are frozen toward their young, and when they fail to make pictures in the mind out of clouds racing across the sky. So long as men can do these things, they can be capable of indignation about the things they should be indignant about; they can be audible about the things they should be talking about, and they can shape their society in a way that does justice to their hopes.

Norman Cousins[10]

---

[10] "The Case For Hope," *Saturday Review*, Dec. 26, 1970, p. 18.

9

What We Must Do!

9–1 The Three Levels of Environmental Awareness

There are three levels of awareness of our ecological crisis. The *first level* is that of discovering the symptom — *pollution*. In only a few years' time the entire country has become acutely aware of pollution, in both its direct and in many of its more subtle forms. Polls now indicate that pollution is one of the major issues for most citizens. While this is most encouraging it is also dangerous. As soon as we discover a problem, we want to fix blame and we want a quick solution. We are now engaged in an unhealthy and counterproductive phase of the environmental crisis — a "pollution witch hunt." In our search for villains we have targeted industry, government, technology, doctors and health officials, the poor, Christianity [1] — anyone, of course, but ourselves. We have not accepted the fact that we are the enemy. Indeed, we must rigorously point out and curtail irresponsible acts of pollution by

---

[1] For an interesting debate on whether the Judaeo-Christian ethic is the villain see Lynn White, Jr., "The Historical Roots of Our Ecological Crisis," *Science*, 155, 1203 (1967); F. Elder, *Crisis in Eden — A Religious Study of Man and Environment*, Abingdon Press, 1970; L. W. Moncrief, "The Cultural Basis for Our Environmental Crisis," *Science*, 170, 508 (1970); R. T. Wright, "Responsibility for the Ecological Crisis," *Bioscience*, 20, 851 (1970); Black, John, *The Dominion of Man*, Aldine, 1970; and Shaeffer, F., *Pollution and the Death of Man*. Tyndale House, 1970.

large or small organizations and resist being duped by eco-pornography.[2] But we must at the same time change our own life styles. We have all been drilling holes in a leaky boat. Arguing over who is drilling the biggest hole only diverts us from working together to keep the boat from sinking.

Another danger in remaining at the pollution awareness level is that it leads people to view the crisis simplistically as a "moon shot" problem. Spend 30-billion dollars and go to the moon; spend 300-billion dollars (the bill is much higher) and clean up the environment. Have technology fix us up, send me the bill at the end of the month, but don't ask me to change my way of living. I hope that you are convinced that using technology and spending enormous amounts of money will be absolutely necessary, but that this will not solve the problem. Hopefully, by dealing with the symptoms, we will buy enough time to deal with the diseases. Dealing only with pollution as a solution to our environmental ills is like trying to cure cancer with band-aids and aspirin.

As this becomes more and more apparent over the next 10 to 20 years, we may enter another very dangerous phase of the environmental crisis. Because there is no purely technological cure, people will want to blame technology and perhaps even destroy the machines in a neo-Luddite [3] revolution. If this should occur, it would seriously aggravate the crisis and probably lead to mass starvation in the United States and in the world. We saw earlier in Figure 6-6 that modern agriculture is almost totally dependent on technology, particularly fossil fuels. Technology will be absolutely essential in dealing with the ecological crisis. The problem is not technology, but our unwise use of technology.

Many have already moved to the *second level* of awareness — the overpopullution level. If you ask what causes pollution, the answer seems obvious — people. But it not just people. It is

---

[2] Examples of eco-pornography abound on TV and in magazine ads. The American oil industry likes to remind us they spend a million dollars a day on pollution control. Wonderful until we realize that their sales are more than $200 million a day. They spend a half a cent of each dollar on pollution control. If some industries spent half has much on pollution control as they do on ads telling us about their ecological good deeds, our environment might really improve.

[3] The Luddites were a group of early 19th-century English workmen who destroyed labor-saving machines as a protest.

also their level of consumption and the environmental impact of various types of production; people x per capita consumption x environmental impact = pollution. And as we have seen (refer to Sections 7-1 and 7-6) this model, while helpful, is too simplistic. At the overpopullution level the answers seem obvious. We must simultaneously reduce the number of passengers and their levels and wasteful patterns of consumption.

But this will not happen unless a reasonable number of our leaders and citizens move to the *third and final level* of ecological awareness — the spaceship-earth level. At this level we recognize that pollution and consumption will not be reduced unless there is a major change in our political, economic, social, and ethical systems. We are faced with four unpleasant political and personal choices, each one more unpleasant than the succeeding one. (1) *Voluntary changeover* to spaceship rules by sacrificing some things and freedoms now in order to preserve some freedoms, and possibly even survival; (2) *semi-voluntary changeover* to spaceship rules based on mutually agreed upon incentives, taxes, sanctions, and laws that protect our environment and ourselves from infringement by others. This is, of course, the basis of our common-law system — mutually agreed upon limits that are enforced. At present our rights to clean air, drinkable water, space, beauty, and diversity are not protected or insured by mutually agreed upon laws. They have been assumed as the common property of everyone and as Garrett Hardin [4] has so aptly demonstrated in his article, "The Tragedy of the Commons," whenever everyone is responsible for something, no one is responsible. Without mutually agreed upon limitation and enforcement to prevent people from abusing the commons, it is destroyed; (3) *repression* and almost complete loss of freedom if we don't change or change fast enough and are forced to move into a martial law and rationing system if famine, disease, social unrest or eco-catastrophes occur; and (4) *the death-rate solution* — letting nature take its course with a massive dieback, probably involving billions. The longer we wait the more likely these last two choices become.

---

[4] Garrett Hardin, *Science, 162*, 1243 (1968). Garrett Hardin has consistently provided us with a thoughtful and original analysis of human ecological problems. All of his writings are highly recommended.

The Three Levels of Environmental Awareness:

First level: *Pollution* — Discovering the symptom

Second level: *Overpopullution* — Population times prosperity equals pollution.

Third level: *Spaceship earth level* — The problem is a complex mix of physical, social, political, and economic factors. Everything is connected to everything.

As a result of our space program, almost everyone in our society has the concept of a spaceship etched into his consciousness. We saw earlier (See Section 3-4) how we have likened earth to our man-made spaceships — an arrogant reversal of reality. Some are now beginning to see what drastic changes a true spaceship outlook requires. Others are also seeing that it may force us to accept our finiteness and interdependence with one another, and with nature. If this occurs, it can represent mankind's transition from childhood to adulthood.

9–2 A Spaceship-Earth Program

What we need then is a massive spaceship-earth program to guide us in converting from our present "cowboy rules" to "spaceship rules" over the next 30 to 50 years. Such a program can not just be another "Manhattan project" or "moon shot" based on the assumption that with money and technology we can accomplish anything — our "Apollo Syndrome." The problem we face now is far more complex. It will require a massive and organized effort of the world's best minds from all fields to determine our priorities, to determine what are the rules for living on a spaceship, to develop social innovations [5] along with technological innovations, to determine what "tire patches" or "band-aids" must be put on now to give us the time needed to make fundamental changes

[5] For an informative analysis of social innovation see K. W. Deutsch, John Platt, and D. Senghaas, "Conditions Favoring Major Advances in Social Science," *Science,* 171, 450 (1971).

in our economic, political, and technological institutions. It will, of course, take enormous amounts of money, but mostly it will take ecological awareness, conscience, and cooperative action on the part of individual citizens.

What would be the nature of such a program? No one really knows but a tentative outline of a spaceship-earth program might involve the following:

A Spaceship Earth Program [6]

1. Identify the major causes of our ecological crisis.

2. Set up a worldwide ecological monitoring and early warning system, perhaps as elaborate as our missile defense system.[7]

3. Begin to formulate the rules for living on a spaceship.

4. Identify short-range problems and institute temporary band-aids to buy the necessary time.

5. Develop and begin instituting careful plans for the long-range transition (perhaps 30 to 50 years) to spaceship rules. Each proposal should be evaluated for scientific, political, administrative, and economic feasibility, ethical acceptibility, and effectiveness along the lines suggested by Bernard Berelson.[8]

6. Move progressively as needed from voluntary methods to incentives to legal restrictions coupled with a massive awareness and persuasion program. Monitoring of the success of each phase should be set up to determine when or if it will be necessary to move to the next level in order to prevent catastrope.

7. Bring about a value revolution — a caring explosion.

---

[6] This author and a colleague, Professor George A. Fouke, and 35 students have been engaged in developing a spaceship earth program, much of which is summarized in this chapter. P. R. Ehrlich and R. L. Harriman have published a plan to save spaceship earth entitled, *How To Be A Survivor,* Ballantine Books, Inc., 1971.

[7] Under the earth resources satellite program NASA will soon orbit a satellite capable of detecting pollutants from a height of 492 miles. A number of such satellites connected to computers could form the basis for a global monitoring system. See Dickson, P. A., "Sensitive Remote Eyes Show Changes on Mother Earth," *Smithsonian,* Jan., 1971, pp. 14-20.

[8] B. Berelson, "Beyond Family Planning," *Science, 163,* 533 (1969).

9-3 Major Causes of the Environmental Crisis

Much work has already been done on identifying causes. Unfortunately, many flood us with quick and overly simplistic cures to our environmental ills. Each has a particular "culprit" and if we will only deal with that particular "root cause," happy days will be here again.

The major root causes that have been identified appear to be:

Major Causes of the Environmental Crisis

1. *Overpopulation:*
   a. Relative to food — underdeveloped countries
   b. Relative to resource consumption and pollution — overpopullution in developed countries.

2. *Population distribution* — the population "implosion," or urban crisis.

3. *Overconsumption and wasteful patterns of consumption* — throwaway society, planned obsolescence, producing unnecessary and harmful items, consuming more than one's fair share of resources, very little recycling of essential resources.

4. *Unwise use of technology* — failing to take into account the impact of our activities on the environment, ignoring the Second Law of Thermodynamics, asking only can we do something not should we do it, blind faith in technology.

5. *Crisis in management* — the failure of our political and economic systems, the growth mania, or bigger is always better syndrome, slow response of government, a counterpunch society lurching from crisis to crisis with no long-range planning, misplaced priorities and refusal to establish spaceship priorities.

6. *Oversimplification of the ecosystem* — failure to observe ecosystem stability through maintaining ecological diversity, wiping out species, failure to recognize that everything is connected to everything.

7. *I-centered behavior* — tragedy of the commons, lack of responsibility for present and future passengers and for the condition of the ship, being now-centered, acting only as a passenger rather than a crew member, gloom and doom, fatalistic and something will turn up cop-outs, the enemy is the other guy.

As the famous mathematician and philosopher Alfred North Whitehead said, "Seek simplicity but distrust it." Hopefully, you now recognize that there is no simple or quick cure. The causes are all connected in a complex, synergistic manner that is not understood. All of these causes (and any others we may discover) must be dealt with *simultaneously* on both a short-range and a long-range approach. Focusing almost exclusively, as we are now doing, on the symptom of pollution hopefully buys a little time. But doing only this, or focusing on only one cause, insures an even more serious and perhaps fatal outbreak later, as we saw in Section 7-6 on world models.

Much more research along the lines pioneered by Forrester and Meadows needs to be done. How are the major causes interrelated? Are they all multiplicative? Are some additive? How should each factor be weighted in terms of time required for change, present and future impact? In Figure 9-1, I have indicated a very crude

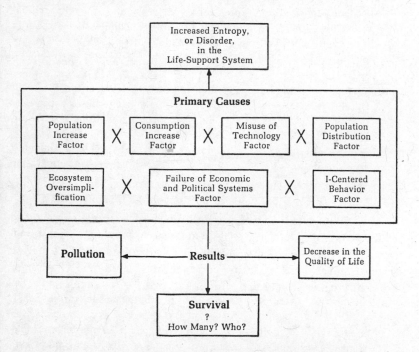

Figure 9–1   A very crude cybernetic model of major causes and results of the ecological crisis on spaceship earth.

cybnernetic model to remind us that all of these factors (and others) are interconnected.

9–4 What We Must Do

Our spaceship is in trouble, so what must we do? No one has a definitive set of answers, but it is possible to outline some suggestions for debate, thought and action. The important thing is not to rely exclusively on one approach.

Summary of What We Must Do

1. *Reduce the number of passengers* — defuse the population bomb by sharply decreasing the birth rate.

2. *Redistribute the passengers* — defuse the population implosion.

3. *Reduce consumption rates and patterns and recycle critical materials* — the first thing the threatened Apollo 13 astronauts did was to cut back on power consumption.

4. *Develop a spaceship governmental system and a steady-state economy.* Growth mania and the nation-state are eventually incompatible with spaceship living.

5. *Preserve ecological diversity* — learn to live in harmony with nature instead of trying to conquer it.

6. *Bring about a caring explosion* — learn to care about the ship and our fellow passengers, those here now as well as those to come.

What follows is a list of possible ways of accomplishing these goals. It is presented, not as a final or complete set of solutions, but as a framework for thinking, debate, and action. The list in general moves from voluntary to involuntary methods. The longer we wait the more likely the solutions near the end of each list.

1. *Reduce the Number of Passengers*

   — The United States being the richest nation, leading consumer of the world's resources, and biggest polluter should set the example for the rest of the world.

— Middle- and upper-class Americans, who are the largest consumers and polluters, should have no more than two children; and preferably one or none until our population is stabilized.

— Adopt a national population policy to attain zero population growth in the United States within 30 years and in the world within 50 years.

— Sharply curtail immigration into the United States.

— A massive TV and other media persuasion and education program to reduce family size. Emphasize that it is the quality not quantity of parenthood that is essential.

— Spaceship-earth curriculum including population dynamics and control introduced into our educational system from kindergarten through college.

— Extensive adult education program with population dynamics as part of job training.

— Primary emphasis on all education, persuasion, or incentive programs on middle and upper classes, who have 10 to 20 times more impact on the environment than the poor.

— Establish a new Department of Population and Environment to determine optimum population and plan and monitor the effectiveness of all programs.

— Heavy tax on household pets that consume protein needed by malnourished humans.

— Crash research program to develop improved birth-control methods that work for years and can be reversed.

— Free birth-control devices and free legalized abortion and sterilization for all citizens.

— Expand family planning but do not depend solely on it because its primay aim is to help couples have the number of children they want when they want them. The problem is that too many people want too many children relative to the ship's capacity to provide them with food, water, and air.

— A new medical ethic. To save lives in the long run, each life prolonged or saved now ethically obligates medical and health personnel to prevent or persuade couples from having children. To restore balance we probably need to prevent four births for each life saved.

— Economic incentives: $500 bonus per year to each woman not having a child until age 30 and to women between 30 and 50 who have no more than two children; no income tax for poor who do not have a child during a given year; income-tax deductions only for a maximum of two children; extra deduction for each year a couple does not have a child.

— Guaranteed annual income to all poor families regardless of number of children, since most taxes and penalties penalize the children in poor families.

— Storefront health, birth-control, welfare, and legal-aid units in neighborhoods, supported by a vast fleet of mobile units bringing these services to the people.

— Plan for a new age structure. U.S. society with a stabilized population (some 60 to 100 years from now) will have an altered age structure, with more old and fewer young people. Transition to this type of society should be planned carefully. In terms of maintaining the steady state required on a spaceship, this type of age structure should be most beneficial, as some Scandinavian and European countries have demonstrated.

— Normally, foreign aid should not be given to a country unless it has instituted a national plan for population control that has a reasonable chance of success.

— If persuasion and incentives do not work, mutually agreed-upon, nonvoluntary methods may have to be introduced, for example, child licenses. The right to have as many children as one wants is in conflict with the right and necessity to have breathable air and drinkable water. After all, the number of husbands or wives each of us can have at one time is limited by law.

2. Redistribute the Passengers

— The immediate pollution problems are primarily local not global. Eco-catastrophes would probably first occur in urban areas. In the United States 70 percent of the people are living on 1 to 2 percent of the land and urban areas are doubling in population at the same rate as India. One new city for 250,000 Americans must be created every 30 days just to keep up with present growth, much less overhaul our decaying cities.

— Establish new cities of 100,000 to 250,000.

— Use McHarg's ecological approach for land-use planning.

— Use bonuses, income-tax reductions, jobs, low-cost housing, and other incentives to encourage industries and people to move to new areas that can support more people.

— Don't fall into the trap of thinking that the only real population problem in the United States is distribution. Redistributing passengers relieves localized population and pollution pressures, but total resource depletion and pollution is not altered significantly — it is merely spread out.

— Most of our vast sparsely populated areas are uninhabitable for large numbers of people. Alaska, Oregon, Nevada, Utah, Idaho, North Dakota, Wyoming, Montana, West Virginia and Maine cannot support large numbers of people because of climate, topography, accessibility and lack of resources. It may be easier and it is certainly cheaper to get citizens to have fewer children than to get them to move to other areas.

— Use cybernetic modeling to determine where people and industries should be located for best use of resources and least detrimental impact.

— Education of city governments, Chamber of Commerce, and citizens on the desirability of deliberately limiting growth. Oregon is already doing this.

— If voluntary and incentive methods don't work, eventually migration into certain areas of the country may have to be prohibited by law and residents in certain critical areas may be required to move to other less densely populated areas.

3. *Reduce the Level and Patterns of Consumption and Recycle Critical Materials*

— Crash program to develop methods for evaluating short-

and long-term impact of all products and technological projects on the environment.

— Assume all chemicals and products are guilty until proven innocent and establish a worldwide monitoring and testing system to establish innocence or guilt. Our constitution does not guarantee chemicals the same rights as people.

— A crash research program to develop more effective pollution control and methods for recycling. The ideal container is a beer bottle made out of pretzels. Recycling paper (60 percent was recycled in the United States during World War II) would reduce our massive solid waste problem by 60 to 80 percent and eliminate much devastation of forests (50 percent recycling would save 92-million acres of forest land each year) and decrease water and air pollution from paper-making industries. Recycling a stack of newspapers only 36 inches high saves one oxygen-producing tree. Aluminum is a triple pollution threat. The aluminum can, a prime example of an item that adds nothing to the quality of our life is a nearly indestructible form of solid waste. Furthermore aluminum production consumes about 6 to 10 percent of all industrial power use in this country — a massive insult to our air and water.[9]

— Bonuses and tax deductions to industries developing new pollution control and recycling methods during the next 10 to 15 years. Base the next industrial revolution on the idea that everything must be recycled. Think of garbage as "urban ore."

— Strong penalties for water and air pollution — rigidly enforced. Make it nonprofitable to pollute.

— Transfer SST, highway trusts, and other "frontier" funds to developing a new automobile engine and to mass transportation systems. The provost of the Massachusetts Insti-

---

[9] Committee on Environmental Information, "The Space Available," *Environment*, March, 1970, p. 5.

tute of Technology has estimated that each U.S. automobile costs the public at large about a dollar per mile when you consider the social costs of displaced land, traffic safety, upkeep of streets and highways, pollution and health.

— Alter our packaging methods. Packages inside of packages are undesirable. Emphasize reusable containers such as grocery and shopping tote bags as used in Europe; return to the reusable metal or plastic lunch pail; milk and soft drinks in bottles, not cartons and cans.

— Reducing our suicidal increase in electricity. Many Europeans live quality lives at half of our electrical output. The eventual costs in pollution, misery, and bad health of increasing our power consumption far outweigh the need for continuing our wasteful and extravagant use of power.

— Institute the necessary laws and enforcement to achieve the goal stated by President Nixon in his 1970 State of the Union address in which he said,

"We can no longer afford to consider air and water common property, free to be abused by anyone without regard to the consequences. Instead we should begin now to treat them as scarce resources which we are no more free to contaminate than we are free to throw garbage in our neighbor's yard. This requires comprehensive new regulations. It also requires that to the extent possible the price of goods should be made to include the cost of producing and disposing of them without damage to the environment."

— Redirect growth by paying the true cost for all products and on all manufacturing, municipal, and agricultural activities. This true cost would include the cost of environmental degradation when the product is made, the cost of making and distributing (our present price system), and the cost of recycling or disposing. This would show everyone the real cost of the things we buy. Research on recycling and minimizing environmental impact would be stimulated, planned obsolescence would be sharply curtailed, growth of some industries and activities would be stimulated while other more harmful ones would be leveled off or deceased by the market mechanism. It would become profitable not to pollute — the reverse of our present system. Part of the extra costs to consumers would be returned by the decrease in bills for health, pollution, cleaning, painting and other hidden effects we are now paying for. For example, the national garbage bill in 1970 was 3-billion dollars, more than that spent on any public service other than schools and roads; emphysema is our fastest growing disease and is responsible for 25,000 to 50,000 deaths per year;[10] air pollution costs a family of four from $300 to $800 per year while the total 1969 Congressional outlay for air pollution control was 45¢ per person;[11] according to the World Health Organization excessive noise costs Americans $4-billion dollars a year in health expenditures and lost pay — loss of hearing at high frequencies is becoming an American characteristic; the total bill for cleaning up the environment between 1970 and 1975 is about $105 billion — an average annual bill of $17.5 billion;[12] 50 percent reduction in air pollution would reduce the nation's health costs by 2-billion dollars annually;[13] over a long holiday weekend Americans throw away enough litter to fill a fleet of garbage trucks 43 miles long — with each bottle, can, or piece of trash costing us about 30 to 60 cents to remove.

— Emphasis should be on reducing energy and resource consumption by the middle and upper classes.

— Institute controls to promote the wise use of technology. Determine the short- and long-term potential environmental impact of all projects including the preservation of

[10] *Air Pollution Control Primer*, National Tuberculosis and Respiratory Disease Assoc., 1969, p. 71.

[11] Berland, T., "Our Dirty Sky," *Today's Health*, A.M.A., XLIV, March, 1966, pp. 40-45.

[12] Goldman, M. I., "The Costs of Fighting Pollution," *Current History*, August, 1970, pp. 73-81.

[13] Lave, L. B., and Seskin, E. B., "Air Pollution and Human Health," *Science, 169*, 723 (1970).

ecological diversity. Don't do some things even if we can do them.

— To discourage use, raise costs of power and water (both too cheap for their impact on environment). No energy source is clean, especially if traced to the power plant. Reverse the present rate structure so largest users will no longer pay lowest price.

— Ration energy consumption and entropy production to limit power production and pollution. For every high entropy-producing convenience (car, airconditioning, and so on) you must give up another one. Plants, individuals, and particular areas or cities might be given only so many energy and entropy units.

— Tax on entropy production by individuals and industries.

— Only one automobile allowed per family or price of second car ten times higher.

— Transfer highway funds to mass transit systems. All new highways for buses only.

— Laws requiring all bottles, cans, paper products, and products using nonrenewable or critical resources to be recycled.

4. *Develop a Spaceship Governmental System and a Steady-State Economic System*

— Establish a Department of Population and Environment or a Department of Long-Range Planning to guide and co-ordinate the changeover to spaceship rules.

— Institute careful long-range planning instead of a short-term crisis response to problems. Anticipate and prevent problems through cybernetic approach rather than counterpunching.

— Reorganize government at all levels to make it more responsive (but not overly responsive); a cybernetic system fluctuating within realistic limits.

— A new bill of rights including environmental rights to clean air, water, and so forth.

— Move towards regional and world governments.

— Add social and environmental costs to the price for all products.

— Guaranteed annual income to prevent poor from bearing real brunt of pollution and other taxes. Part of increased taxes recycled to the poor.

— Face up to the fact that many minority group members considered the population-pollution movement a form of genocide for the poor and oppressed minority groups. Far too many white upper- and middle-class Americans see the U.S. population problem as one of saturating the ghettos with birth-control programs. Remember that in terms of pollution the typical middle-class American family with three children is equivalent to a poor family with from 30 to 50 children. Many poor Americans, perhaps legitimately, feel that the environmental movement is a cruel hoax. They argue that they would be glad to be concerned about pollution if they could just become affluent enough to pollute. Democratic party chairman Lawrence O'Brien asks in a recent speech, "What priority does air pollution have to a mother in the core city whose baby has been bitten by a rat? What priority does a polluted lake have to a family whose main recreation area is a littered alley?" We must find the resources to deal with poverty and environmental problems simultaneously. This will probably require some form of guaranteed annual income.

— Crash program of research by top economists to design steady-state economic systems and plan an orderly transition to the new system over the next 30 years. A stabilized population and economic system does not mean economic stagnation. It means redirected growth based on

---

[14] For an outline of how to accomplish both goals see Robert Theobald, *The Economics of Abundance*, Pitman, 1972; Robert Theobald, *Habit and Habitat*, Prentice-Hall, 1972; and Warren Johnson and John Hardesty, *Economic Growth vs The Environment*, Wadsworth, 1971.

quality rather than quantity. Economists must save themselves and the rest of us by becoming ecologized.[15]

— A fundamental reordering of priorities deemphasizing the arms race and defense spending. World military expenses have escalated from 1-billion dollars at the end of World War II to 200-billion dollars in 1970. The United States now spends 8-million dollars per hour on defense and a thousand times less on environment. In total cost, one prototype bomber is equivalent to 75 fully equipped, 100-bed hospitals; one atomic submarine equals 10,000 high schools; one standard jet bomber equals school lunch for 1-million children.[16]

— Ecology, not pollution, should become our number one election issue. Everyone is in favor of reducing pollution but moving the issue to the overpopullution and spaceship levels requires people to take controversial stands. A new breed of ecologically aware and committed leaders must be put into office at all levels. Ecology, consumer, and other groups should join together rather than being defeated by divide and conquer tactics.

— Education and persuasion program to show that bigger is not always better. The next time someone says we must clear off this land, park or wilderness for an airport or power plant because we are supposed to have 100,000 new pasengers or users of electricity in the next 10 years, ask just one question. Suppose we don't build it? Then we wouldn't have all of those passengers and users crowding into our living space and adding more to our stress, noise,

[15] An increasing number of economists are becoming involved. See Daly, H. E., "Toward a Stationary-State Economy," in Harte, J. and Socolow, R. H., *Patient Earth,* Holt, Rinehart & Winston, 1971, pp. 226-244; Heller, W. W., "Economic Growth and Ecology — An Economist's View," *Monthly Labor Review, 94,* 14 (1971); Ayres, R. U. and Kneese, A. V., "Economic and Ecological Effects of a Stationary Economy," in Johnston, R. F. et al, eds., *Annual Review of Ecology and Systematics, Vol. 2,* Annual Reviews, 1971, Chap. 1; Spengler, J. J., "Economic Growth in a Stationary Population," PRB Selection No. 38, Population Reference Bureau, July, 1971; and the additional references in the bibliography at the end of this book.

[16] For additional cost comparisons see John McHale, *The Ecological Context,* George Braziller, Inc., New York, 1970, p. 27.

and pollution, would we? This does not mean that we should blindly oppose all power plants, airports, or shopping centers. Each project should be evaluated on an individual basis with insistence that environmental impact be minimized and that ecological diversity be preserved.

9–5 What Can You Do?

In the final analysis, it all comes down to what you and I are willing to do on an individual level. We must bring about a caring explosion where we each accept some responsibility as crew members on our ship, rather than acting solely as passengers.

What Can You Do?

1. *Become ecologically informed.*[17] Give up your "cowboy" thinking and immerse yourself in spaceship thinking. Specialize in one particular area of the ecological crisis and pool your specialized knowledge with others. Everyone doesn't need to be an ecologist but you do need to ecologize your particular profession or job.

2. *Sensitize yourself to your environment.* Look around your room, your home, your school and your place of work. What things around you really improve the quality of your life? What ecologically unsound practices are you carrying out?

3. *Live a simpler life style* based on reduced energy consumption. and entropy production. Go on an energy and entropy diet. For every high-energy or entropy thing you do (having a child, buying a car, living or working in an airconditioned building) give up a number of other things. Such a life style will be cheaper and it may add more joy as we learn how to break through the plastic technological cocoon that separates us from nature and from one another.

4. *Above all, become politically involved on a local and national level.* Start or join a local environmental group and also join a national organization.[18] Become the David Brower, Ralph Nader,

---

[17] See the detailed bibliography at the end of this book.

[18] For example, Zero Population Growth, Friends of the Earth, The Sierra Club, Common Cause, Ralph Nader's Center for the Study of Responsive Law, and the Environmental Defense Fund. The addresses of these and a number of additional environmental organizations are found at the end of this book (pp. 184–185).

Paul Ehrlich, Rachel Carson, Barry Commoner, or John Gardner of your block or school. Use synergy to amplify your results. We would see major improvements in the environment if each of use set aside $30 per year and donated $5 to six politically active environmental organizations. Hire professional lobbyists and lawyers to work for you.

5. *Remember that environment begins at home.*[19] Before you start converting others begin by changing your own living patterns. Be prepared for the fact that if you become an ecological activist everyone will be looking for and pointing out your own ecological sins.

6. *Avoid the extrapolation to infinity syndrome* as the usual excuse for not doing anything — the idea that if we can't change the entire world quickly then we won't change any of it. While most people sit on the bank waving their hands over how difficult the system is to change, others (e.g., Ralph Nader) go ahead and change it by doing their homework and by using the system to change the system.

7. *Do the little things.*[20] It is all of the little things, the individual acts of consumption, litter and so on, that got us into the mess. When you are tempted to say this little bit won't hurt, multiply it by 207,000,000 Americans saying the same thing. Undoing all the little things is the only way out. Picking up a single beer can, not turning on a light, writing on both sides of a piece of paper, not buying a grocery product with packages inside of packages, are all very significant acts. Each small act reminds us of ecological thinking and leads to other ecologically sound practices. The secret of beginning is to begin. Start with a small concrete personal act, and expand outward into ever-widening circles. Steadily whittle away at making fundamental changes in our entire political, economic, and social system over your lifetime. But simultaneously do a number of small band-aid actions to keep the ship together while it is being overhauled. These specific acts also help you avoid psychic numbness of despair at the awesome magnitude of the job to be done. We must work step by step.

---

[19] To appreciate what this really means read the superb book by Mark Terry, *Teaching for Survival,* Ballantine Books, Inc., 1971 (paperback). Anyone who is really concerned with what to do should read this book.

[20] For detailed suggestions of what you can do see the list of books in the "What Can You Do" section of the bibliography at the end of this book.

8. *Work on the big polluters* — primarily through political action. Individual actions help reduce pollution, give us a sense of involvement, and most important help us develop a badly needed ecological consciousness. However, this awareness must then expand to recognize that large scale pollution occurs as a result of some industries, municipalities and big agriculture.

9. *Start a reverse J-curve of awareness and action.* The world is changed by changing the two people next to you. For everything — big or little — that you decide to do, make it your primary goal to convince two others to do the same thing and convince them in turn to convince two others. Carrying out this doubling process only 28 times would convince everyone in the United States; you only need to persuade about 5 to 10 percent for action. After 32 doublings everyone in the world would be convinced.

10. *Don't make people feel guilty.* Treat everyone as a unique human being. If a couple has a number of children or someone is overconsuming don't make them feel bad. Instead, find the things that each individual is willing to do to help our environment. There is plenty to do and no one can do everything. Use positive rather than negative reinforcement.

The secret of sustained action is to think and work on two levels simultaneously. On a long-range basis we must continually whittle away at making major changes in our political and economic systems and our world view. At the same time we must do a number of little daily things at the band-aid level, to give us the time needed for the major changeover to a steady-state world. Daily accomplishments also give us the psychic energy to keep working on long-range changes, where progress will be slow.

Begin at the individual level and work outward in ever widening circles. Join with others and amplify your actions. Remember that with care and skill two plus two can be greater than four. This is the way the world is changed.

Indifference is the essence of inhumanity.

George Bernard Shaw

Epilogue

This book is based on nine deceptively simple theses:

1. That the ecological crisis is not only more complex than we think but more complex than we can ever think.

2. That, in Garrett Hardin's terms, the basic principle of ecology is "that everything and everyone are all interconnected." Truly accepting this and trying to learn how things are interconnected will require a fundamental change in our patterns of living.

3. That on a closed spaceship there are no consumers — only users of materials. We can never really throw anything away.

4. That because of the First Law of Thermodynamics we cannot get something for nothing and because of the Second Law of Thermodynamics, almost every action of man has some undesirable impact on our environment or life-support system. As a result, there is ultimately no completely technological solution to pollution on a spaceship — although technology can help. A continued increase in the number of passengers and their levels and wasteful patterns of the use of energy and materials must insure a continuing decline in the quality of life and threaten survival for a large number of the passengers.

5. That because we have rounded the bend on a "J," or exponential, curve of increasing population, use of resources and energy, and pollution, man for the first time has the potential to seriously disrupt his life-support system.

6. That the implication of all of these almost obvious ideas is that *each of us* and particularly those in the affluent middle and upper classes, must now give up certain things and patterns in our lives in order to prevent a continuing decrease in freedom and in the quality of life. We may live to experience the future we deserve.

7. That our primary task must be to transform from arrogant, linear thinking to circular, cybernetic thinking that is in harmony with the ecological cycles that sustain us.

8. That informed action based on hope that transcends gloom and doom pessimism, blind technological optimism, and apathy now provides mankind its greatest opportunity to come closer to that elusive dream of peace, freedom, brotherhood, and justice for all passengers.

9. It is not too late, if . . . There is time — 30 to 50 years — to deal with these complex problems if enough of us really care. It's not up to "them," but it is up to "us." Don't wait!

When there is no dream, the people perish.

Proverbs

Selected Bibliography

The Problems

1. Edberg, R., *On the Shred of a Cloud*. University of Alabama Press, 1969.
2. Ehrlich, P. R., *The Population Bomb*. New York: Ballantine Books, 1968.
3. King-Hale, D., *The End of the Twentieth Century*. New York: St. Martin's, 1971.
4. Linton, R. M., *Terracide — America's Destruction of Her Living Environment*. Boston: Little, Brown & Co., 1970.
5. Rienow, R. and Rienow, L. T., *Man Against His Environment*. New York: Ballantine Books, 1970.
6. Rienow, R. and Rienow, L. T., *Moment in the Sun*. New York: Ballantine Books, 1969.
7. Taylor, G. R., *The Doomsday Book*. New York: World Publishing Co., 1970.

Ecology

1. Billings, W. D., *Plants, Man, and the Ecosystem*. Belmont, Calif.: Wadsworth Publishing Co., 1970.
2. Dasman, R. F., *Environmental Conservation*, 2nd ed. New York: John Wiley, 1968.
3. Ehrenfeld, D. W., *Biological Conservation*. New York: Holt, Rinehart & Winston, 1970.
4. Farb, P., *Ecology*. New York: Time, Inc., 1970.
5. Grossman, Shelley, *Understanding Ecology*. New York: Grosset & Dunlap, 1970.
6. Joffe, J., *Conservation*. Garden City, N.Y.: Natural History Press, 1970.

7. Kormandy, E. J., *Concepts of Ecology*. Englewood Cliffs, N.J.: Prentice-Hall, 1969.

8. Marx, W., *The Frail Ocean*. New York: Ballantine Books, 1967.

9. Odum, E. P., *Ecology*. New York: Holt, Rinehart & Winston, 1963.

10. Odum, E. P., *Fundamentals of Ecology*, 3rd ed. Philadelphia: W. B. Saunders, 1971.

11. Owen, O. S., *Natural Resource Conservation, An Ecological Approach*. New York: Macmillan, 1971.

12. Reid, K., *Nature's Network*. Garden City, N.Y.: Natural History Press, 1969.

13. Scientific American, *The Biosphere*. San Francisco: W. H. Freeman, 1970.

14. Segerberg, O., *Where Have All the Flowers, Fishes, Birds, Trees, Water, and Air Gone?* New York: David McKay Co., 1971.

15. Smith, R. L., *Ecology and Field Biology*. New York: Harper & Row, 1966.

16. Teal, J. and Teal, M., *Life and Death of a Salt Marsh*. New York: Ballantine Books, 1969.

Human Ecology and Ethics

1. American Friends Service Committee, *Who Shall Live?* New York: Hill and Wang, 1970.

2. Augenstein, L., *Come Let Us Play God*. New York: Harper & Row, 1969.

3. Black, John, *The Dominion of Man: The Search for Ecological Responsibility*. Chicago: Aldine, 1970.

4. Boughey, A. S., *Man and the Environment*. New York: Macmillan, 1971.

5. Boulding, Kenneth E., *The Meaning of the 20th Century*. New York: Harper & Row, 1964.

6. Brown, M., ed., *The Social Responsibility of the Scientist*, New York: Macmillan, 1971.

7. Carson, R., *Silent Spring*. Boston: Houghton-Mifflin, 1962.

8. Carvell, F. and Tadlock, M., *It's Not Too Late*. Beverly Hills, Calif.: Glencoe Press, 1971.

9. Chase, S., *The Most Probable World*. New York: Harper & Row, 1968.

10. Commoner, B., *The Closing Circle: Nature, Man, and Technology*. New York: Alfred A. Knopf, 1971.

11. Darling, F. F. and Milton, J. P., eds., *Future Environments of North America*. Garden City, N.Y.: Natural History Press, 1966.

12. Dasman, R. F., *A Different Kind of Country*. New York: Macmillan, 1968.

13. Disch, R., ed., *The Ecological Conscience*. Englewood Cliffs, N.J.: Prentice-Hall, 1970.

14. Dubos, René, *Reason Awake — Science for Man*. New York: Columbia University Press, 1970.

15. Dubos, René, *So Human an Animal*. New York: Charles Scribner's Sons, 1970.

16. Ehrlich, P. R. and Ehrlich, A. H., *Population, Resources and Environment*. San Francisco: W. H. Freeman, 1970.

17. Elder, F., *Crisis in Eden: A Religious Study of Man and Environment*. Nashville, Tenn.: Abingdon Press, 1970.

18. Falk, R. A., *This Endangered Planet*. New York: Random House, 1971.

19. Forrester, J. W., *World Dynamics*. Cambridge, Mass.: Wright-Allen Press, 1971.

20. Fromm, E., *The Revolution of Hope*. New York: Harper & Row, 1968.

21. Gardner, J. W., *The Recovery of Confidence*. New York: W. W. Norton, 1970.

22. Hall, E. T., *The Hidden Dimension*. Garden City, N. Y.: Doubleday, 1966.

23. Hamilton, M., ed., *This Little Planet*. New York: Charles Scribner's Sons, 1970.

24. Harrison, G., *Earthkeeping*. Boston: Houghton-Mifflin, 1971.

25. Heiss, R. L. and McInnis, N. F., *Can Man Care for the Earth?* Nashville, Tenn.: Abingdon Press, 1971.

26. Henshaw, P. S., *This Side of Yesterday*. New York: John Wiley, 1971.

27. Majumder, S., *The Drama of Man and Environment*. Columbus, Ohio: Charles E. Merrill, 1971.

28. McHale, John, *The Ecological Context*. New York: George Braziller, 1970.

29. McHarg, I. L., *Design With Nature*. Garden City, N.Y.: Natural History Press, 1969.

30. Meadows, D. H., Meadows, D. L., Randers, J., and Behrens, W., *The Limits to Growth: A Global Challenge*. New York: Universe Books, 1972.

31. Mines, S., *The Last Days of Mankind*. New York: Simon and Schuster, 1971.

32. Potter, V. R., *Bioethics: Bridge to the Future*. Englewood Cliffs, N.J.: Prentice-Hall, 1971.

33. Ryan, W., *Blaming the Victim*. New York: Pantheon Books, 1971.

34. Scoby, D. R., *Environmental Ethics*. Minneapolis: Burgess, 1971.

35. Shaeffer, Francis, *Pollution and the Death of Man.* Wheaton, Ill.: Tyndale House, 1970.

36. Shepherd, P. and McKinley, D., eds., *The Subversive Science: Essays Toward an Ecology of Man.* New York: Houghton-Mifflin, 1969.

37. Wagner, R. H., *Environment and Man.* New York: W. W. Norton & Co., Inc., 1971.

Population and Agriculture

1. Bogue, D. J., *Principles of Demography.* New York; John Wiley, 1969.

2. Borgstrom, G., *The Hungry Planet.* New York: Collier, 1965.

3. Borgstrom, G., *Too Many, A Study of Earth's Biological Limitations.* New York: Macmillan, 1969.

4. Brown, L. R., *Seeds of Change: The Green Revolution and Development in the 1970's.* New York: Praeger, 1970.

5. Chasteen, E. R., *The Case for Compulsory Birth Control.* Englewood Cliffs, N.J.: Prentice-Hall, 1971.

6. Commission on Population Growth and the American Future, "Population Growth and the American Future," Interim report, March, 1971, U. S. Government Printing Office, Washington, D.C.

7. *Control of Pesticides.* Geneva: World Health Organization, 1970.

8. Day, L. H. and Day, A. T., *Too Many Americans.* New York: Delta, 1965.

9. Dumont, R. and Rosier, B., *The Hungry Future.* New York: Praeger, 1969.

10. Fraser, D., *The People Problem.* Bloomington: University of Indiana Press, 1971.

11. Hardin, G., ed., *Population, Evolution and Birth Control.* San Francisco: W. H. Freeman, 1969.

12. Lader, L., *Breeding Ourselves to Death.* New York: Ballantine Books, 1971.

13. National Academy of Sciences, *Rapid Population Growth: Consequences and Policy Implications,* Vol. I and II. Baltimore: Johns Hopkins, 1971.

14. Paddock, W. and Paddock, P., *Famine — 1975!* Boston: Little, Brown, 1967.

15. Petersen, W., *Population,* 2nd ed. New York: Macmillan, 1969.

16. Pohlman, E., *How to Kill a Population,* Philadelphia: Westminster Press, 1971.

17. Rodale, J. I. and Staff, *Our Poisoned Earth and Sky.* Emmaus, Pa.: Rodale Press, 1971.

18. Rodale, R. ed., *The Basic Book of Organic Gardening.* New York: Ballantine Books, 1971.

19. Rudd, R. L., *Pesticides and the Living Landscape*. Madison: University of Wisconsin Press, 1964.

20. Thompson, W. S. and Lewis, D. T., *Population Problems*. New York: McGraw-Hill, 1964.

21. Westoff, L. A. and Westoff, C. F., *From Now to Zero. Fertility, Contraception and Abortion in America*. Boston: Little, Brown, 1971.

Pollution

1. *Air Pollution Control Primer*. Scientific Services Corp., 750 Summer St., Stamford, Conn. ($5.00).

2. American Chemical Society, *Solid Wastes*. Washington, D.C.: American Chemical Society, 1971.

3. Baron R. A., *The Tyranny of Noise*. New York: St. Martin's, 1971.

4. Carr, D. E., *The Breath of Life*. New York: W. W. Norton, 1965.

5. *Cleaning Our Environment: The Chemical Basis for Action*. Washington, D.C.: American Chemical Society, 1969.

6. Commoner, B., *The Closing Circle: Nature, Man and Technology*. New York: Alfred A. Knopf, 1971.

7. Cooper, D. F. and Jolly, W. C., *Ecological Effects of Weather Modification*. Ann Arbor: University of Michigan, School of Natural Resources, 1969.

8. Hamblin, L., *Pollution — The World Crisis*. New York: Barnes and Noble, 1971.

9. Montague, K. and Montague, P., *Mercury*. New York: Sierra Club, 1971.

10. Report of the Study of Critical Environmental Problems, *Man's Impact on the Global Environment*. Cambridge, Mass.: The MIT Press, 1970.

11. Report of the Study of Man's Impact on Climate (SMIC), *Inadvertent Climate Modification*. Cambridge, Mass.: The MIT Press, 1971.

12. Small, W. E., *Third Pollution: The National Problem of Solid Waste Disposal*. New York: Praeger, 1971.

13. Stewart, G. R., *Not So Rich As You Think*. Boston: Houghton-Mifflin, 1967.

14. Strobble, M. A., ed., *Understanding Environmental Pollution*. St. Louis: Mosby, 1971.

15. Treshow, M., *Whatever Happened to Fresh Air?* Salt Lake City: University of Utah Press, 1971.

16. Turk, A., Turk, J., and Wittes, J. T., *Ecology, Pollution and Environment*. Philadelphia: W. B. Saunders, 1972.

17. Warren, C. E., *Biology and Water Pollution Control*. Philadelphia: W. B. Saunders Co., 1971.

18. Wilber, C. G., *The Biological Aspects of Water Pollution*. Springfield, Ill.: Charles C. Thomas, 1969.

19. Willrich, T. L. and Hines, N. W., eds., *Water Pollution Control and Abatement*. Ames: Iowa State University Press, 1967.

Economics

1. Behan, W. and Weddle, R. M., eds., *Ecology, Economics and Environment*. Missoula, Montana: University of Montana Press, 1971.

2. Berkley, P. W., and Seckler, D. W., *Economic Growth and Environmental Decay*. New York: Harcourt Brace Jovanovich, 1972.

3. Crocker, T. O. and Rogers, A. J., III, *Environmental Economics*. Hinsdale, Ill.: Dryden Press, 1971.

4. Dales, J. H., *Pollution, Property and Prices*. Toronto: University of Toronto Press, 1968.

5. Editors of Fortune, *The Environment*. New York: Harper & Row, 1970.

6. Galbraith, J., *The Affluent Society*. New York: Mentor, 1969.

7. Galbraith, J., *The New Industrial State*. New York: Signet, 1967.

8. Goodman, M. I., *Controlling Pollution — The Economics of a Cleaner America*. Englewood Cliffs, N.J.: Prentice-Hall, 1967.

9. Jarrett, H., ed., *Environmental Quality in a Growing Economy*. Baltimore: Johns Hopkins, 1966.

10. Johnson, W. and Hardesty, J., *Economic Growth vs. The Environment*. Belmont, Calif.: Wadsworth, 1971.

11. Kneese, A. V., Ayres, R. V., and D'ange, R. C., *Economics and the Environment*. Washington, D.C.: Resources for the Future, 1970.

12. Meier, R. L., *Science and Economic Development*, 2nd ed. Cambridge, Mass.: MIT Press, 1966.

13. Mishan, E. J., *Technology and Growth — The Price We Pay*. New York: Praeger Publishers, 1969.

14. Samuelson, P. A., *Economics: An Introductory Analysis*, 7th ed. New York: McGraw-Hill, 1967.

15. Spencer, M. H., *Contemporary Economics*. New York: Worth, 1971.

16. Theobald, R., *The Economics of Abundance*. New York: Pitman Publishing, 1970.

17. Theobald, R., *Habit and Habitat*. Englewood Cliffs, N.J.: Prentice-Hall, 1972.

Energy and Resources

1. Brown, T. V., *Energy and Environment*. Columbus, Ohio: Charles E. Merrill, 1971.

2. Bryerton, G., *Nuclear Dilemma*. New York: Ballantine Books, 1970.

3. Clawson, M., ed., *Natural Resources and International Development*. Baltimore: Johns Hopkins, 1965.

4. Cloud, Preston E., Jr., ed., *Resources and Man*. San Francisco: W. H. Freeman, 1969.

5. Curtis, R. and Hogan, E., *Perils of the Peaceful Atom*: The Myth of Safe Nuclear Plants. New York: Doubleday & Co., 1969.

6. Fisher, J. L. and Potter, N., "Resources in the United States and the World," in Hauser, P. M., ed., *The Population Dilemma*. Englewood Cliffs, N.J.: Prentice-Hall, 1963.

7. Goffman, J. W. and Tamplin, A. R., *Poisoned Power*. Emmaus, Pa.: Rodale Press, 1971.

8. Landsberg, H. H., Fischman, L. L. and Fisher, J. L., *Resources in America's Future*. Baltimore: Johns Hopkins, 1963.

9. Novick, S., *The Careless Atom*. Boston: Houghton-Mifflin, 1969.

10. Odum, H. T., *Environment, Power and Society*. New York: John Wiley, 1971.

11. Park, C. F., Jr., *Affluence in Jeopardy*. San Francisco: Freeman-Cooper, 1968.

12. Pincus, J. H., ed., *Reshaping the World Economy: Rich and Poor Countries*. Englewood Cliffs, N.J.: Prentice-Hall, 1968.

13. Publications of Resources for the Future, Inc., 1755 Massachusetts Ave., N.W., Washington, D.C. 20036.

14. Seaborg, G. T. and Corliss, W. R., *Man and Atom: Building a New World Through Nuclear Technology*. New York: E. P. Dutton, 1971.

15. Skinner, B. J., *Earth Resources*. Englewood Cliffs, N.J.: Prentice-Hall, 1969.

16. Watt, K. E. F., *Ecology and Resource Management*. New York: McGraw-Hill, 1968.

17. Wright, J., *The Coming Water Famine*. New York: Coward-McCann, Inc., 1966.

Politics

1. Anderson, W., ed., *Politics and Environment*. Pacific Palisades, Calif.: Goodyear Publishing Co., 1970.

2. Caldwell, L., *Environment: A Challenge for Modern Society*. Garden City, N.Y.: Natural History Press, 1970.

3. Chamberlain, N. W., *Beyond Malthus: Population and Power*. New York: Basic Books, 1970.

4. Cooley, R. A. and Wandesforde-Smith, Geoffrey, eds., *Congress and the Environment*. Seattle: University of Washington Press, 1970.

5. Davies, J. C., *The Politics of Pollution*. New York: Pegasus, 1970.

6. de Bell, G., ed., *The Voter's Guide to Environmental Politics*. New York: Ballantine Books, 1970.

7. Fabricant, N. and Hallman, R. M., *Toward a National Power Policy: Energy, Politics and Pollution*. New York: Braziller, 1971.

8. Graham, Frank, Jr., *Disaster by Default, Politics and Water Pollution*. New York: M. Evans & Co., 1966.

9. Landau, N. J. and Rheingold, P. D., *The Environmental Law Handbook*. New York: Ballantine Books, 1971.

10. Perloff, H. E., ed., *The Future of the U.S. Government: Toward the Year 2000*. New York: Braziller, 1971.

11. Ridgeway, J., *The Politics of Ecology*. New York: Dutton, 1970.

12. Roos, L. L., Jr., ed., *The Politics of Ecosuicide*. New York: Holt, Rinehart & Winston, 1971.

Thermodynamics

1. Angrist, S. W. and Hepler, L. G., *Order and Chaos*. New York: Reinhold, 1965.

2. Baker, J. J. W. and Allen, G. E., *Matter, Energy and Life*, 2nd ed. Reading, Mass.: Addison-Wesley, 1970.

3. Firth, D. C., *Elementary Chemical Thermodynamics*. London: Oxford University Press, 1969.

4. Lehinger, A. L., *Bioenergetics*, 2nd ed. New York: Benjamin, 1971

5. Miller, G. T., *Energetics, Kinetics and Life — An Ecological Approach*. Belmont, Calif.: Wadsworth Publishing Co., 1971.

6. Pimentel, G. C. and Spratley, R. D., *Understanding Chemical Thermodynamics*. San Francisco: Holden-Day, 1969.

7. Thompson, J. J., *An Introduction to Chemical Energetics*. New York: Houghton-Mifflin, 1967.

What Can You Do?

1. Adams, A. B., *Eleventh Hour*. New York: Putnam, 1970.

2. Bock, A., *The Ecology Action Guide*. Los Angeles: Nash Publishing, 1971.

3. Cailliet, G., Stezer, P. and Love, M., *Everyman's Guide to Ecological Living*. New York: Macmillan, 1971.

4. Carvell, F. and Tadlock, M., *It's Not Too Late*. Beverly Hills, Calif.: Glencoe Press, 1971.

5. de Bell, G., ed., *The Environmental Handbook*. New York: Ballantine Books, 1970.

6. de Bell, G., ed., *The Voter's Guide to Environmental Politics*. New York: Ballantine Books, 1971.

7. *Do-It-Yourself Ecology.* Environmental Action, 2000 P St., N.W., Washington, D.C. 20036 (25¢).

8. Ehrlich, P. R. and Harriman, R. L., *How to be a Survivor.* New York: Ballantine Books, 1971.

9. Goldstein, J., *How To Manage Your Company Ecologically.* Emmaus, Pa.: Rodale Press, 1971.

10. Landau, N. J. and Rheingold, P. D., *The Environmental Law Handbook.* New York: Ballantine Books, 1971.

11. Love, S., ed., *Earth Tool Kit.* New York: Pocket Books, 1971.

12. Saltenstall, R., *Your Environment and What You Can Do About It.* New York: Walker & Co., 1971.

13. Sax, J. L., *Defending the Environment.* New York: Alfred A. Knopf, 1971.

14. Sickle, D. V., *The Ecological Citizen.* New York: Harper & Row, 1971.

15. Swatek, P., *The User's Guide to the Protection of the Environment.* New York: Ballantine Books, 1971.

16. Terry, M., *Teaching for Survival.* New York: Ballantine Books, 1971.

Anthologies of Important Articles

1. Anderson, P. K., ed., *Omega: Murder of the Ecosystem and Suicide of Man.* Dubuque, Iowa: Wm. C. Brown Co., 1971.

2. Blau, S. D. and Rodenbeck, J. von B., *The House We Live In — An Environmental Reader.* New York: Macmillan, 1971.

3. Chute, R. M., *Environmental Insight.* New York: Harper & Row, 1971.

4. Cox, G. W., ed., *Readings in Conservation Ecology.* New York: Appleton-Century Crofts, 1969.

5. Detwyler, T. R., ed., *Man's Impact on Environment.* New York: McGraw-Hill, 1971.

6. Ehrlich, P. R. and Holdren, J. P., eds., *Global Ecology: Readings Toward a Rational Strategy for Man.* New York: Harcourt Brace Jovanovich, 1971.

7. Ehrlich, P. R., Holdren, J. P. and Holm, R. W., eds., *Man and the Ecosphere.* San Francisco: W. H. Freeman, 1971.

8. Hardin, G., ed., *Population, Evolution, and Birth Control.* San Francisco: W. H. Freeman, 1969.

9. Harte, J. and Socolow, A. H., *Patient Earth.* New York: Holt, Rinehart & Winston, 1971.

10. Helfrich, H. W., Jr., ed., *Agenda for Survival.* New Haven, Conn.: Yale University Press, 1970.

11. Helfrich, H. W., Jr., ed., *The Environmental Crisis.* New Haven, Conn.: Yale University Press, 1970.

13. Jackson, Wes, *Man and the Environment*. Dubuque, Iowa: Wm. C. Brown, 1971.

13. Johnson, H. C., ed., *No Deposit — No Return*. Palo Alto, Calif.: Addison-Wesley, 1970.

14. Leisner, R. S. and Kormondy, E. J., eds., *Ecology*. Dubuque, Iowa: Wm. C. Brown, 1971.

15. Leisner, R. S. and Kormondy, E. J., eds., *Pollution*. Dubuque, Iowa: Wm. C. Brown, 1971.

16. Leisner, R. S. and Kormondy, E. J., eds., *Population and Food*. Dubuque, Iowa: Wm. C. Brown, 1971.

17. Mergen, F., ed., *Man and His Environment: The Ecological Limits of Optimism*. New Haven, Conn.: Yale University Press, 1970.

18. Murdoch, W. W., ed., *Environment: Resources, Pollution and Society*. Stamford, Conn.: Sinauer Associates, Inc., 1971.

19. Novick, S. and Cottrell, D., eds., *Our World in Peril: An Environmental Review*. Greenwich, Conn.: Fawcett Publications, Inc., 1971.

20. Reville, R., Khosla, A. and Vinovskis, eds., *The Survival Equation*. Boston: Houghton-Mifflin, 1971.

Periodicals

1. *BioScience*. American Institute of Biological Sciences: Washington, D.C.

2. *C. F. Newsletter*. Conservation Foundation, 1717 Massachusetts Ave., N.W., Washington, D.C. 20036. ($6/yr.)

3. *Environment*. Committee for Environmental Information, 438 N. Skinker Blvd., St. Louis, Mo. 63130 ($8.50/yr.)

4. *Environment Action Bulletin*. 33 E. Minor St., Emmaus, Pa. 18049 ($10/yr.)

5. *Environmental Science and Technology*. American Chemical Society, 1155 16th St., N.W., Washington, D.C. 20036 ($7/yr.)

6. *Population Bulletin*. Population Reference Bureau, 1755 Massachusetts Ave., N.W., Washington, D.C. 20036 ($3/yr.)

7. *Science*. American Association for the Advancement of Science: Washington, D.C. ($12/yr.)

8. *Science for Society — A Bibliography*. An annual bibliography on environment published by the American Association for the Advancement of Science, Education Department, 1515 Massachusetts Avenue, N.W., Washington, D.C. 20005 (95¢)

Environmental Organizations

1. Center for the Study of Responsive Law, 1908 Q Street, N.W., Washington, D.C. 20009 (Ralph Nader).

2. Common Cause, 2100 M Street, N.W., Washington, D.C. 20037.

3. Conservation Foundation, 1250 Connecticut Ave., N.W., Washington, D.C. 20036.

4. Consumer Alliance, Inc., P. O. Box 1242, Los Altos, Calif. 94022.

5. Environmental Action, Inc., Room 731, 1346 Connecticut Ave., N.W., Washington, D.C. 20036.

6. Environmental Defense Fund, Inc., P. O. Box 740, Stony Brook, N.Y. 11790.

7. Friends of the Earth, 30 E. 42nd St., New York, N.Y. 10017.

8. Izaak Walton League of America, 1326 Waukegan Road, Glenview, Ill. 60025.

9. John Muir Institute for Environmental Studies, 451 Pacific Ave., San Francisco, Calif. 94133.

10. League of Conservation Voters, 917 Fifteenth St., N.W., Washington, D.C. 20005.

11. League of Women Voters Education Fund, 1730 M Street, Washington, D.C. 20036.

12. National Audobon Society, 1130 Fifth Ave., New York, N.Y. 10038.

13. National Wildlife Federation, 1412 16th Street, N.W., Washington, D.C. 20036.

14. Nature Conservancy, The, 1522 K St., N.W., Washington, D.C. 20005.

15. Planned Parenthood, 515 Madison Ave., New York, N.Y. 10022.

16. Population Crisis Committee, 1730 K St., N.W., Washington, D.C. 20006.

17. Population Reference Bureau, 1755 Massachusetts Ave., Washington, D.C. 20036.

18. Rachel Carson Trust for the Living Environment, Inc., 8940 Jones Mill Road, Washington, D.C. 20015.

19. Resources for the Future, Inc., 1145 19th St. N.W., Washington, D.C.

20. Scientist's Institute for Public Information, 30 W. 68th St., New York, N.Y. 10021.

21. Sierra Club, 1050 Mills Tower, San Francisco, Calif. 94104.

22. Wilderness Society, The, 729 15th St., N.W., Washington, D.C. 20005

23. Zero Population Growth, 367 State St., Los Altos, Calif. 94022.

Index

Figure = (f), Footnote = (n), Table = (t)

Abortion: (see also Population control)
  legalize, 161
AEC (see Atomic Energy Commission)
Africa:
  alligator:
    importance of, 90
  hippopotamus:
    importance of, 87, 90
Age structure, 17–24, 32, 142, 162
  curves, 22, 22(f)
  India, 23
  in stationary state society, 32, 32(t)
  underdeveloped countries, 21, 22(f),
    23(t)
  U. S., 20, 21(f), 22(f), 23(t)
  world, 21, 22(f), 23(t) (see also
    Population, Population dynamics,
    and Population growth)
Agriculture, 100–116
  animal feedlots and pollution of lakes,
    75–82, 78(f), 81(f)
  and DDT, 93–95, 95(f) (see also DDT)
  decrease in farm population, 34
  ecological effects of, 45, 48, 96–97,
    113–116, 114(f), 114(n), 116(n)
  and ecosystem simplification, 96–97
  and fertilizer pollution of lakes, 75–82,
    78(f), 81(f)
  fertilizer use, 75, 116
  and fossil fuels, 114, 114(f)
  green revolution, 2, 113–114, 114(n)
  growing more food, 2, 100–116
  growing more food is not enough,
    113–116
  loss of topsoil, 76, 108
  and population growth, 37, 37(f)
  and Second Law of Thermodynamics,
    107–116
  and water, 108–109, 108(n) (see also
    Food)
Air pollution:
  from automobiles, 79–80, 123, 123(f)
  brown-air cities, 79–80
  costs, 166, 166(n)
  emission control devices, 80
  emphysema, 166, 166(n)
  future projections, 123, 123(f)
  greenhouse effect, 69–72, 72(n)
  gray-air cities, 79–81
  hydrocarbons, 80
  London, 80

Los Angeles, 79–80
New York, 80
  nitrogen oxides, 79–80
  oxides of nitrogen, 79–80
  particulates, 72, 72(n), 80
  photochemical smog, 80
  smog, 80
  sulfur dioxide, 80–81
Algae:
  bloom, 77, 129 (see also Eutrophication
    and Nitrogen cycle)
  as food, 105
Alienation, 6, 145
Alligator, 87, 90
Aluminum:
  and electric power consumption,
    164, 164(n)
  recycling, 164
  supply of, 128(t)
Anderson, L., 34(n)
Animal(s):
  as component of ecosystems, 63–64,
    65(f)
  extinction of, 1, 87
  feedlots, 78–79, 78(f), 81(f), 116 (see
    also Nitrogen cycle)
  wastes, 78–79, 78(f), 81(f), 116 (see
    also Eutrophication and Nitrogen
    cycle)
  as source of water pollution, 78–79,
    78(f), 81(f)
Apollo space mission, 41
Apollo syndrome, 156
Arms race, 1, 169
Asia, grain diet of, 105
Aswan Dam, ecological effects of, 91
Atmosphere: (see also Air pollution)
  carbon dioxide content, 71
  cooling of, 72, 72(n)
  disruption of climate, 67–72
  dust in, 72
  greenhouse effect, 69–72, 72(n)
  heating up of, 67–72, 72(n), 131, 131(n)
  ignorance of long-term effects, 72,
    72(n)
  nitrogen content, 74
  particulate matter in, 72
  and solar energy, 58
  thermal pollution, 131, 131(n)
Atomic Energy Commission (AEC), 130
Automobile (see Motor vehicles)

Awareness:
  of ecological crisis, 150–151, 153–156,
    170 (see also Ecological crisis)
Ayres, R. U., 169(n)

Backlash, ecological, 90–93, 93(n)
Bacteria:
  in an ecosystem, 63–64 (see also
    Decomposers)
  in nitrogen cycle, 74–75
Berelson, Bernard, 25(n), 157, 157(n)
Berland, T., 166(n)
Biogeochemical cycles (see Chemical
    cycles)
Biological amplification, 93–95, 95(f)
Biological magnification, 93–95, 95(f)
Biomes, 63
Biosphere, 58–59, 62–63
  components of, 58–59, 59(f)
  as a cybernetic system, 83
  energy flow, 69–72
Birth control: 26(n) (see also
    Population control)
  information availability, 31
  research, 161
Birth rate(s), 8, 8(n), 16–17, (see also
    Population, Population control and
    Population dynamics)
  crude, 8(n), 17, 18(f), 19(f)
  and death rate, 9
  in developed countries, 18(f)
  must be lowered, 40–41
  net, 8, 8(n), 9
  U.S., 18, 20–21
  in underdeveloped countries, 18(f)
  world, 19(f)
Black Americans:
  genocide issue, 168, 168(n)
  and population growth, 122, 122(n),
    168, 168(n)
Black, John, 153(n)
Borgstrom, Georg A., 106, 106(n)
Borlaug, N. E., 114(n)
Borman, F. H., 13(n)
Borneo:
  ecological effects of using DDT, 91
Boulding, Kenneth, 13, 13(n)
Brady, N. C., 77(n)
Breeder reactors, 129 (see also Nuclear
    power and Nuclear fission)
Broecker, W. S., 73(n)
Brower, David, 151, 170
Brown, Lester R., 114(n), 116, 116(n)

California:
  loss of farm land, 108, 108(n)
Cambel, A. B., 131(n)
Campbell, J. Arthur, 132, 132(t), 132(n)
Carbon cycle, 68–73, 70(f)
  diagram of, 70(f)
  disruption of, 71–72, 72(n)

and fossil fuels, 70–72, 70(f)
and photosynthesis, 69
and respiration, 69
Carbon dioxide: (see also Air pollution
    and Greenhouse effect)
  buildup in atmosphere, 67–72, 67(n),
    72(n)
  content in atmosphere, 71
  greenhouse effect, 67–72, 67(n), 72(n)
  recycling rate, 67
  and thermodynamics, 48
Carnivores, 64 (see also Ecosystem)
Carrying capacity, 35–37, 37(f) (see also
    Population, Population dynamics,
    and Population growth)
  man's ability to raise, 36–38
Carson, Rachel, 171
Cells, living, 47–48
Census Bureau, 20, 27(t), 28(t), 32(t),
    33, 122
Change, social, 150
Chardin, Teilhard de, 53, 146
Charlier, R. H., 125(n)
Chemical cycles, 60, 68–82, 68(n)
  in biosphere, 59–61, 60(f)
  carbon, 68–73, 70(f)
    disruption of, 69–72
  disruption of, 66–68, 71, 75–81
  and ecosystems, 63–66, 65(f)
  nitrogen, 74–82, 74(f)
  oxygen, 68–73, 70(f)
Chicago, air pollution, 80
Children:
  cost of, 26, 26(t) (see also Population
    control)
  number per family, 23–32 (see also
    Fertility rate)
  number wanted per family, 31
  psychology of having, 27, 27(n)
  quality of parenthood, 26
  reasons for having, 27, 27(n)
China, raising mother's age at first
    child, 33(n)
Chlorophyll, 58
Christianity, as cause of ecological
    crisis, 153, 153(n)
Climate:
  modification, 67–72, 67(n) (see also
    Air pollution, Atmosphere, Green-
    house effect, Carbon dioxide,
    Particulate matter)
Closed system(s), 5, 51, 52–53 (see also
    Thermodynamics)
Coal, 127
  sulfur dioxide pollution, 80–81
  supply of, 128(t)
Coale, Ansley J., 120(n)
Commission on Population Growth and
    the American Future, 26, 26(n), 34
Common Cause, 146, 151

Commoner, Barry, 12, 12(t), 12(n), 118(n), 119(t), 120, 120(n), 171
Community, 62 (see also Ecosystem)
Computer simulation:
  of world ecosystem, 86–87, 86(n), 89(f), 134–143 (see also Cybernetics)
Conservation of energy (see Thermodynamics, First Law of)
Consumers, 63 (see also Ecosystem)
  in an ecosystem, 63–64
  macro, 63–64
  micro, 63–64
Consumption:
  bomb, 12–13
  and GNP, 12, 12(t), 13
  and pollution, 12(t), 117–123
  and population growth, 12–13, 12(t), 118–121, 118(t), 118(n), 119(t)
  reduction of, 163–167
  wasteful patterns in U. S., 3, 158
Copper:
  supply of, 128(t)
Corr, M., 12(n), 119(t), 120(n)
Corliss, W. A., 126(n)
Costs:
  of having children in U.S., 26, 26(t)
Cousins, Norman, 133(n), 152, 152(n)
Cox, Harvey, 41
Coyote:
  side effects of U. S. extermination program, 91
Cousteau, Jacques, 111, 111(n)
Crocodile:
  ecological importance, 90
Cultural eutrophication, 77 (see also Nitrogen cycle)
Cybernetics, 83–87, 134–143
  and biosphere, 83
  complex systems, 85–86, 134–143
  and computer simulation, 86–87, 134–143
  diagram, 84(f)
  ecosystem models, 134–143
    limitations of, 141–142
  fedback, 83–84
  homeostatic plateau, 35(f), 36, 85, 85(f) (see also Carrying capacity and S-Curve)
  and human thinking, 143
  information feedback, 83–84
  and land use planning, 98–99
  models for population redistribution, 163
  negative feedback, 84
  overload of system, 85
  positive feedback, 84
  and synergy, 85–86
  temperature control in living organisms, 84
  thermostat, 83–84, 84(f)

and world ecosystem simulation, 86–87, 86(n), 89(f), 134–143
Cybernetic system(s), 83
  counter to normal thinking, 85, 143
Cycling of Chemicals (see Chemical cycles)

Daly, H. E., 142(n), 169(n)
Davis, Kingsley, 34(n)
Davis, Wayne H., 122, 122(n)
DDT, 16–17, 93–95, 95(f)
  benefits of, 91
  biological magnification, 93–95, 95(f)
  concentration in humans, 94
  food chain magnification, 94–95, 95(f)
  and malaria control, 93
  and population growth, 17
  problems with, 91–93
Death:
  from malnutrition, 2, 40, 40(n)
  from past world disasters, 11(t)
  and Second Law of Thermodynamics, 48
  from starvation, 2, 40, 40(n)
Death rate(s), 8, 8(n), 9, 16–17
  crude, 8, 8(n), 17, 18(f)
  in developed countries, 18(f)
  may rise, 40
  net, 8, 8(n), 9
  in underdeveloped countries, 18(f)
  U.S., 19
  world, 19(f)
Decomposers (see also Ecosystem)
  in ecosystem, 63–64
Deevy, E. S. Jr., 37(f)
Demographers, 8(n), 24, 24(n) (see also Population, Population dynamics, and Population growth)
Demography (see Population dynamics)
Department of Population and Environment, 161, 167
Dependency load:
  reduced by ZPG, 32
Desalination of water, 109
Detergents:
  and eutrophication of lakes, 78, 78(f), 79(n), 81–82, 81(f)
  how to stop using, 125(n)
  and phosphates, 78, 78(f), 79(n), 81–82, 81(f)
Deutsch, K. W., 156(n)
Developed countries:
  birth rates, 18(f)
  children per family, 24
  death rates, 18(f)
  energy consumption, 127, 127(n)
  overpopulation in, 3, 117
  thermodynamic revolutions, 133–134
  use of resources by, 1, 2, 3, 117, 117(n), 121–122, 121(n)
Dickson, P. A., 157(n)

Disease:
 emphysema, 166, 166(n)
 and population growth, 41
 schistosomiasis, 90–91
Disorder (see Thermodynamics and
  Second Law of Thermodynamics)
 and entropy, 49–51
 increasing, 46–51
 and Second Law of Thermodynamics,
  46–51
 and solar energy, 48
Diversity:
 cultural, 1
 in ecosystems, 1, 87, 90–93, 96–97,
  98–99, 160
 and ecosystem stability, 87, 90–93,
  96–97, 96(n), 98–99
 importance of, 1, 87, 90–93, 160
Doubling time (see also Population,
  Population dynamics, and Population
  growth)
 defined, 2, 10
 Mexico, 24
 Turkey, 34
 of U.S. industrial growth, 13
 of U.S. population, 13
 of world population, 10(t)
Dubos, René, 82, 147, 147(n)
Dumont, R., 40(n)
Dust (see also Air pollution and
  Atmosphere)
 air pollution, 80

Earth (see also Spaceship Earth)
 arrogance towards, 53
 as a closed system, 5, 49
 history of population growth, 37
 life support system, 1
 misuse of term "spaceship earth,"
  51–53
 as a spaceship, 1, 5, 13, 49
Eastlund B. J., 130(n)
Ecological awareness, 150, 153-156, 170
 levels of, 153–156
 need for, 170
 overpopullution level, 154–156
 pollution level, 153–154, 156
 spaceship earth level, 155–156
 use of media, 161
Ecological backlash, 90–93, 93(n)
Ecological crisis:
 as arrogance towards nature, 51–53
 awareness of, 150, 153–156, 170
 causes of, 117–121, 117(n), 118(n),
  120(n), 153–156, 158–159, 159(f)
 citizen groups, 151, 171, 184–185
 cybernetic models, 1, 86–89, 134–143,
  159(f)
 description of, 5, 6
 education, 161

effect of reducing birth rate, 136,
  137(f), 138(f), 140(f)
effect of reducing pollution, 135
  136(f), 136, 138(f), 140(f)
effect of reducing use of resources,
  135, 136(f), 136, 138(f), 140(f)
as an entropy crisis, 54–55
and The Greening of America, 148–149
hope, 145–152
individual action, 170–172, 182–183
and industrialization, 117–121, 142–143
Judaeo-Christian ethic as cause, 153,
  153(n)
levels of awareness, 153–156
myth of single causes, 121, 153–156,
  158–160, 159(f)
nature of, 3
no simple causes, 121, 153–156, 158–160,
  159(f)
optimism, 146, 151
and overpopulation (see Population,
  Population dynamics, and Population growth)
pessimism, 146–147
and Second Law of Thermodynamics,
  49–55, 147, 173
solutions, 134–143, 153–172
 summary, 160
symptoms of, 6
and thermodynamics, 49–55, 147, 173
time left to deal with our problems,
  3, 4, 14
value revolution, 157, 160
and values, 143
Ecological diversity, 1, 87, 90–93, 96–97,
  160
Ecological effects:
 of electric power, 131(f)
Ecological monitoring:
 chemicals, 164
 systems, 157, 157(n)
Ecological myths, 107–116
Ecological pyramids, 101–102, 102(f),
  104(f), (see also Food chain)
Ecological side effects, 87, 90–93, 93(n)
Ecology, 61
 goals of, 63
 ignorance about, 97
 and land use planning, 97–99
 principle of, 63
Economic growth:
 limiting of, 163
 redirect, 165–166
Economics:
 cost of raising children, 26
 and energy crisis, 126–127
 guaranteed annual income, 162, 168
 implications of zero population
  growth, 31, 31(n), 32, 168(n), 169(n)
 incentives for pollution control, 162,
  164

reduce growth, 163–167
remove tax deductions, 162
social costs, 165–166, 166(n), 168
steady-state, 142, 142(n), 167–168, 168(n), 169(n)
Eco-pornography, 154, 154(n)
Ecosphere (see Biosphere)
Ecosystem, 61–68
  animals in, 63–64
  backlash, 90–93, 93(n)
  carnivores, 64
  and chemical cycling, 63–66, 65(f) (see also Chemical cycles)
  components of, 63–66, 65(f)
  consumers in, 63–64
  cybernetic models of, 86–87, 134–143
  as cybernetic system, 83, 121
  and DDT, 91–95 (see also DDT)
  decomposers, 63–64
  disruption of carbon cycle, 70–72
  disruption of chemical cycles, 66–82
  disruption of energy flow, 66–72
  disruption of nitrogen cycle, 74–82, 78(f), 81(f)
  diversity, 90–93, 96–97, 96(n), 98–99, 160
  energy flow in, 63–66, 65(f), 100–105, 101(n), 101(f), 102(f), 104(f), 131, 131(n)
  food chain, 100–102, 101(n), 101(f), 102(f), 104–105
  food web, 103, 103(f)
  function, 61–68
  herbivores, 64
  macroconsumers, 63–64
  microconsumers, 63–64
  omnivores, 65
  plants, 63–64, 66
  problems in, 66–68
  producers in, 63–64
  productivity of, 110, 110(n)
  pyramid of numbers, 101–102, 102(f), 104–105, 104(f)
  and Second Law of Thermodynamics, 64, 66–67, 69–72
  simplification by man, 96–97, 98–99
  and solar energy, 57–66, 65(f)
  stability, 83, 88, 90–93, 96–97, 96(n), 98–99
  steady state in, 66, 83, 148
  structure, 63–66, 65(f)
  trophic levels, 66
  types of, 63
  what can go wrong, 66–68, 71–73, 75–82
Edberg, Rolf, 99
Eddington, Arthur S., 56
Education:
  illiteracy increasing, 111, 111(n)
  in population dynamics needed, 161
  and protein deficiency, 105–106, 105(n), 112

Efficiency (see also Thermodynamics)
  and energy crisis, 130
  fuel cells, 130
  of internal combustion engine, 54
  of photosynthesis, 58
  of steam engine, 54, 130
  thermodynamic, 45, 54
Egypt:
  ecological effects of Aswan Dam, 91
Ehrlich, Anne H., 40(n)
Ehrlich, Paul R., 8, 8(n), 40(n), 73, 73(n), 96, 116, 117, 117(n), 120(n), 157(n), 171
Eichenwald, H. F., 105(n)
Elder, F., 153(n)
Electric car, pollution problems, 125
Electricity (see also Energy crisis)
  rise cost of, 167
  reduce use of, 165
Electric power (see also Energy crisis)
  ecological effects 128–131, 130(f)
Emission control devices, 80 (see also Air pollution and Motor vehicles)
Emphysema, 166, 166(n)
Enke, Stephen, 31, 31(n)
Energy:
  conservation of, 43–45, 45(f), 107 (see also First Law of Thermodynamics)
  consumption, 127, 127(n)
  crisis, 126–133, 126(n), 127(n), 130(n), 131(n), 132(t) (see also Energy crisis)
  degradation of, 50, 64–66, 100–104 (see also Second Law of Thermodynamics)
  and ecosystems, 63–66, 65(f), 100–104
  flow in an ecosystem, 59–61, 60(f), 69–72, 65(f), 100–104 (see also Energy flow)
  geothermal, 130
  heat (see Heat and Thermal pollution)
  kinetic, 44
  law of conservation of, 43–45 (see also Thermodynamics, First Law of)
  nuclear (see Nuclear energy and Nuclear power)
  potential, 43, 44
  solar, 57–59, 126, 130
  use in U. S. 126
Energy crisis, 126–133, 165–166
  causes, 128
  ecological effects, 131(f)
  economic issues, 127
  geothermal energy, 130
  increasing efficiency as a solution, 130
  moral issues, 127
  nuclear fusion, 130, 130(n)
  nuclear power plants, 129–131, 130(n), 131(f)
  political issues, 127

projected consumption, 127
projected consumption, 127–128
reducing use as a solution, 165–166
solar energy, 130
Energy flow:
  disruption of, 66–68, 71–72, 131, 131(n)
  in an ecosystem, 59–61, 60(f), 65–66,
    65(f), 100–104
  in food chain, 100–102, 101(f), 101(n),
    102(f), 104–105, 104(f)
Environment: (see also Surroundings,
  Second Law of Thermodynamics,
  Life-support system)
  impact on by Americans, 3, 12–13,
    117–123
  industrial revolution, 38
  and Second Law of Thermodynamics,
    49–55
Environmental awareness, 153–156
  (see also Ecological crisis and
  Ecological awareness)
Environmental bill of rights, 168
Environmental crisis (see Ecological
  crisis)
Environmental organizations, 151,
  170(n), 184–185
Entropy: (see also Second Law of
  Thermodynamics)
  and death, 48
  defined, 49
  as disorder, 49
  and ecological crisis, 54–55
  and environmental crisis, 54–55, 147,
    173
  increasing, 49–51
  and overpopulation, 121
  and Second Law of Thermodynamics,
    49
  tax on production of, 167
Estuaries:
  eutrophication in, 79(n)
  preservation of very important, 110
  productivity of, 110, 110(n)
Eutrophication, 76–82, 77(n), 78(f), 79(n),
  81(f) (see also Nitrogen cycle)
  causes of, 77–78, 77(n), 78(f)
  cultural, 77, 77(n)
  and phosphates, 78, 78(f), 81–82
  solutions, 81–82, 81(f)
Everglades, importance of alligator to,
  90
Evolution:
  not a solution to pollution, 112
Exponential growth (see also J-curve)
  meaning of, 2, 3, 6–8, 36(n), 37(n)
Extermination of species, 1, 87

Falk, R. A., 31(n)
Family planning: (see also Population
  control)

limitations of, 31, 161
number of children wanted is too
  great, 31
Famines, 11, 11(t), 40, 40(n)
Farm population in U. S., 34 (see also
  Agriculture and Food)
Favor, M. T., 93(n)
Fawcett, J. T., 27(n)
Feedback, 83 (see also Cybernetics)
  loops, 84–85, 87
  negative, 84
  positive, 84
Feedlots: (see also Animal wastes,
  Eutrophication and Nitrogen cycle)
  and water pollution, 75–82, 78(f),
    81(f), 115, 116
Fertility rate, 24–34 (see also Population
  dynamics and Population growth)
  general, 24(n)
  total, 24, 24(n)
  U.S., 27, 27(t)
Fertilizer: (see also Eutrophication,
  Nitrates and Nitrogen cycle)
  artificial, 75
  ecological effects, 116
  and eutrophication of lakes, 75–82,
    78(f), 81(f)
  increase in use of, 76, 116
  runoff, 75–82
  use to increase crop yields, 75
First Law of Thermodynamics, 43–45, 55,
  107 (see also Thermodynamics)
Fisher, Joseph L., 121(n)
Fission (see Nuclear fission)
Flow of energy: (see Ecosystem and
  Energy flow)
Food, 100–116
  algae as, 105
  chains, 100–102, 101(n) (see also
    Ecosystem)
  and DDT, 93–94, 94(f)
  defined, 100–101, 101(f)
  and energy flow, 100–102, 101(n),
    101(f), 102(f), 104–105, 104(f)
  and Second Law of Thermody-
    namics, 100–102, 101(n), 101(f),
    102(f), 104–105, 104(f)
  cultivating more land, 107–108
  decrease in farm population, 34
  ecological effects of growing, 96–97,
    113–116, 114(f)
  and ecosystem simplifiication, 96–97
  famines, 11, 11(t), 40, 40(n)
  and fossil fuels, 114, 114(f)
  and use of fertilizer, 75
  green revolution, 2, 113, 114, 114(n)
  increasing yield, 2, 113, 114, 114(n)
  loss of topsoil, 76, 108
  malnutrition, 2, 74, 106–107 (see also
    Protein)

nutrient leaks from soil, 76
from oceans, 109–110
and overpopulation, 3, 113–117
protein shortage, 2, 74, 106–107 (see
        also Protein)
pyramid (see Food chains)
synthetic, 45, 111
and water, 108–109, 109(n)
web, 103, 103(f)
Foreign aid:
and population control, 162
Forests:
need for, 99
preservation of, 63, 99
Forrester, Jay W., 86–87, 86(n), 89(f),
        121, 134–143, 136(n), 159
Fossil fuels (see also Air pollution)
agricultural use, 114, 114(f)
and carbon cycle, 70–72, 72(f), 72(n)
and greenhouse effect, 67–72
Fouke, George A., 157(n)
Franke, Robert G., 145(n)
Freedom:
to have children question, 40, 162
loss of, 3, 6
Friends of the Earth, 151
Frye, P. C., 105(n)
Fuel cells, efficiency of, 130
Fungi, in an ecosystem, 63–64 (see also
        Decomposers)
Fusion (see Nuclear fusion)
Future shock, 14

Galston, A. W., 92(n)
Garbage costs, 166
Gardner, John W., 146, 146(n), 151
Gecko, 91
Genesis, 144
Genetic information, conservation of, 87
Genocide, and population control, 168,
        168(n)
Geometric growth (see J-curve)
Geothermal energy, 130 (see also Energy
        crisis)
Gloom and doom cop out, 6, 146, 147
GNP: (see also Economics)
and consumption, 12, 12(t), 13
and pollution, 12, 12(t), 13, 118–121
and population growth, 12, 12(t),
        118–121
versus Gross National Quality, 13
Gofman, John W., 126(n)
Goldman, Marshall I., 166(n)
Gough, W. C., 130(n)
Gravity, law of, 42
Great Lakes, 79
Greenhouse effect, 67–72, 67(n) (see also
        Air pollution, Atmosphere and
        Carbon dioxide)
The Greening of America, 148–149,
        148(n)

Green plants, 87
Green revolution, 2, 113–114, 114(n)
Gross National Product (see GNP)
Gross National Quality, 13
Guaranteed annual income, 162, 168
        (see also Economics)

Hardesty, John, 168(n)
Hardin, Garrett, 26, 26(n), 113, 155,
        155(n), 173
Harriman, R. L., 157(n)
Harte, John, 131(n), 142(n), 169(n)
Hauser, Philip M., 24(n), 30(n), 121(n)
Hawaii, ecological effects of predator
        control, 92
Heat pollution, 67–72, 72(n), 129–131,
        131(n) (see also Atmosphere, Energy
        crisis and Thermal pollution)
Heller, Walter W., 169(n)
Herbicides, use in Viet Nam, 92–93, 92(n)
Herbivores, 64 (see also Ecosystem)
Highways, increase in, 108
Highway trust fund, 164
Hippopotamus, importance of in eco-
        system, 87, 90
Holdren, John P., 117(n), 120(n)
Homeostatic plateau: (see also Cyber-
        netics and S-curve)
defined, 36, 85
diagram, 85(f)
and S-curve, 35(f), 36, 37, 37(f)
Houghton, H., 111(n)
Housing, lack of in world, 10
Hulett, H. R., 39(n)
Human values (see Values, human)
Humus, 75–76 (see also Nitrogen cycle)
Hunger, 100–116 (see also Food, Malnu-
        trition and Protein)
degree of in world, 2, 115, 115(n)
lack of protein, 105–106, 106(n)
protein exploitation by developed
        countries, 106–107, 106(n)
and Second Law of Thermodynamics,
        104–105
statistics, 115, 115(n)
UN estimates of, 9, 10, 115 115(n)
Hydrocarbons, 80 (see also Air pol-
        lution)

I-centered behavior, 158
Illiteracy: (see also Education)
increasing, 111, 111(n)
Immigraton: (see also Population dy-
        namics and Population control)
curtailment of in U.S., 31, 161
and U.S. population growth, 19, 19(n),
        28
India, 23
age structure, 23
population growth, 9, 23
Individual action, 170–172, 182–183

Industrial revolution:
  and carbon dioxide in the atmosphere,
    71 (see also Greenhouse effect)
  growth rate in U.S., 13
  negative effects of, 38
  and population growth, 36, 37–38
Information feedback, 83–84 (see also
  Cybernetics)
Inorganic fertilizer (see Fertilizer)
Insecticides (see DDT)
Internal combustion engine: (see also
  Air pollution)
  and air pollution, 79–80
  efficiency very low, 54, 130
I.Q., and protein deficiency, 105, 105(n),
  112
Iron, supply of, 127, 128(t)
Irrigation, and increase in schisto-
  somiasis, 91

J-curve, 2, 6–8, 7(f), 8(f)
  around the bend on, 2, 5, 6, 7, 25
  change to S-curve, 35–41
  of consumption, 12–13
  implications of, 11(t), 13–15
  lag phase, 6
  many types of, 14
  meaning of, 6, 7, 36(n)–37(n)
  of increasing pollution, 3, 4, 12–13
  of population growth, 2, 3, 5, 6
  of resources depletion, 5
  threatens us, 41
Johnson, H. R., 128(t)
Johnson, Warren, 168(n)

Keeton, William T., 103(f)
Keyfitz, Nathan, 10(f)
Kneese, A. V., 169(n)

Lake Erie, 125
Lakes: (see Eutrophication and Nitrogen
  cycle)
  eutrophication of, 75–82, 78(f), 81(f)
Land: (see also Food)
  cultivating more, 107–108
Land use planning, 97–99
  ecological approach, 98–99, 98(n)
Lapp, Ralph E., 126(n)
Law of Conservation of Energy (see
  First Law of Thermodynamics)
Law of Conservation of Matter, 124
Law of Conservation of Pollution,
  124–125
Law of gravity, 42
Law(s):
  scientific, 42–43
  of thermodynamics, 42–56 (see also
    Thermodynamics)
  stated, 43, 49, 51
Lead, supply of, 128(t)

Lewis, D. T., 33(n)
Life, and Second Law of Thermody-
  namics, 47–48
Life-support system, 57–82 (see also
  Environment, Biosphere)
  of earth, 1, 57–59
  impact on by Americans, 3, 12–13,
    117–123
  industrial revolution, 38
  and Second Law of Thermodynamics,
    49–55
  summary of critical problems, 66–68
  threatened, 5
  what can go wrong, 66–68
London, air pollution, 80
Long Island Sound:
  DDT magnification in food chain,
    93–95, 95(f)
Louisiana:
  loss of alligator population, 90
Love, L. B., 166(n)
Luddites, 154(n)
Lyle, David, 108(n)

McHale, John, 10(n), 54(n), 116(n),
  128(t), 169(n)
McHarg, Ian L., 98, 98(n), 163
Malaria:
  control by DDT, 93
Malnutrition: (see also Protein)
  deaths from, 2, 40, 40(n)
  degree of in world, 2, 115, 115(n)
  lack of protein, 105–106, 105(n), 106(n)
  and learning, 105, 105(n), 116
  statistics, 115, 115(n)
  U.N. estimate of, 9, 10
Man:
  effect on ecosystems, 96–97, 98–99
  as omnivore, 64
Maximum population, 3, 38–40, 39(n),
  39(f), 132–133, 132(t), 133(n) (see
  also Population control and Popula-
  lation growth)
Meadows, Dennis, 86–89, 89(n), 89(f),
  134–143, 141(n), 159
Mencken, H. L., 150
Mexico, and population growth, 24
Middle-class Americans:
  biggest polluters, 122, 161
Military expenditures, 169
Miller, J. Irwin, 148, 148(n)
Milton, J. P., 93(n)
Mining, 108, 108(n)
Moncrief, L. W., 153(n)
Mongoose, 92
Monster, J., 79(n)
Montague, Nancy, 89(f)
Moynihan, Patrick, 150
Mother boom in U.S., 20, 21(f), 30–31
  (see also Age structure, Population
  growth and Population dynamics)

Motor vehicles:
  and air pollution, 79–80, 123, 123(f)
  emission control devices, 80
  growth rate of in U.S., 9
  low efficiency of, 54
  as source of water pollution, 78(f), 79, 81, 81(f)
  restriction of ownership, 167

Nader, Ralph, 151, 170
National Academy of Sciences, 25
National park system, 99
Natural gas, 127, 128(t)
Nature, arrogance towards, 53
Negative feedback, 84 (see also Cybernetics)
Neo-Luddite revolution, 154, 154(n)
New York, air pollution, 80
Nitrate: (see also Eutrophication and Nitrogen cycle)
  fertilizer runoff, 75–82
  in nitrogen cycle, 74–75
  overload in lakes, 77–82, 77(n), 78(f), 81(f)
Nitric oxide, 79–80 (see also Air pollution)
Nitrogen content in atmosphere, 74
Nitrogen cycle, 74–82, 74(f)
  disruption of, 75–82
  and eutrophication of lakes, 76–82
  humus in soil, 75
  and lack of protein, 74 (see also Malnutrition)
  in lakes, 77
  nitrates, 74(f), 75
  nitrites, 74(f), 75
Nitrogen dioxide, 79–80 (see also Air pollution)
Nixon, Richard M., 26, 122, 165
Noise pollution, costs, 166, 166(n)
Nonspontaneous processes, 45–46 (see also Thermodynamics)
Nuclear fission, 129 (see also Energy crisis)
Nuclear fusion:
  reactors, 130, 130(n)
  in sun, 48, 57
Nuclear power plants, 129–131 (see also Energy crisis)
Nutrient cycling (see Chemical cycles)
Nutrient leaks (see Nitrogen cycle, disruption of)
Nutrition:
  and learning, 105, 105(n), 112
O'Brien, Lawrence, 168
Ocean:
  food from, 109–110
  photosynthesis in, 73, 73(n)
  pollution of, 73, 73(n), 111, 111(n)
  productivity of, 110, 110(n)
  upsetting ecological balance, 73

Odum, Eugene P., 97, 97(n), 110(n)
Oil, 127, 128(n), 128 (t)
Omnivores, 64, 103 (see also Ecosystem)
Open system, 51, 52 (see also Thermodynamics)
Optimum population, 3, 38–40, 39(n) (see also Population control, Population growth and S-curve)
Order and Second Law of Thermodynamics, 46–51 (see also Entropy)
Organizations, environmental, 151, 170(n), 184–185
Orwell, George, 147
Overpopulation, 16–41 (see also Population, Population control and Population growth)
  in developed countries, 3, 117–123
  and food supply, 3, 100–116
  and middle-class Americans, 122
  and poor Americans, 122–123
  and pollution, 3, 117–121, 117(n), 118(n), 118(t), 119(t), 120(n)
  two types of, 3, 12–13, 117–118
  in underdeveloped countries, 3, 18–19, 22, 25, 34–41, 158
Overpopullution, 117–118, 154–156
Oxides of nitrogen, 79–80 (see also Air pollution)
Oxygen, 70(f)
  cycle, 68–73, 70(f)
  depletion in lakes by eutrophication, 77–78
  from photosynthesis in ocean, 73, 73(n)
  recycling rate, 67
  solubility in water, 129
  supply of, 73, 73(n)

Packaging, wasteful methods of, 165
Paddock, William C., 114(n)
Paper recycling, 164
Particulates (see Air pollution, particulates)
Parts per billion, 93–94, 93(n)
Patchen, Kenneth, 98
PCB's, 94–95
Periodicals, 184
Perry, H., 128(t)
Pest control, 92–93 (see also DDT)
Pesticides: (see also DDT)
  biological magnification, 93–95, 95(f)
  DDT, 91–92, 93–95, 95(f)
Petersen, W., 33(n)
Peterson, Bruce, 101(n)
Pets as protein consumers, 106, 161
Phosphates:
  in detergents, 125, 125(n)
  and eutrophication of lakes, 78–82
Phosphorus, 124, 128(t)
Photochemical smog, 80 (see also Air pollution)

Photosynthesis, 64
  and carbon cycle, 69, 69(n)
  efficiency of, 58
  in oceans, 73, 73(n)
  and Second Law of Thermodynamics,
    48
Phytoplankton, 73, 73(n)
Plague, 11(t)
Plants:
  as components of ecosystems, 63–64,
    66
  extinction of, 1
  and photosynthesis, 64
  use of solar energy, 58
Platt, J. R., 5(n), 156(n)
Politics, 167–168
  ecology as election issue, 169
  and energy crisis, 127
  individual involvement, 170–171
  and population control, 23–24, 25
Pollution: (see also Atmosphere, Air
    Pollution)
  from agriculture, 45, 48, 75–82, 78(f),
    81(f)
  air, 71–72
  from animal wastes, 75–82, 78(f), 81(n)
  from automobile, 79–80, 123, 123(f)
  bomb, 12–13
  can never be eliminated, 124–125
  causes of, 117–121, 117(n), 118(n),
    120(n)
  and consumption, 12(t), 12–13, 117–121
  control:
    costs of cleaning up, 154, 166, 166(n)
    economic incentives, 164
    social costs, 165
  dilution not the solution, 47
  effect of reducing, 138, 139(f), 140(f)
  and evolution, 112
  exponential growth of, 3
  from electricity, 131
  from fertilizer runoff, 75–82, 78(f),
    81(f)
  and GNP, 12, 12(t), 119–120
  growth of rate in U.S., 13
  heat, 129–131, 131(n) (see also Thermal
    pollution)
  increase of, 3, 4, 13
  J-curve, 3, 4
  law of conservation of, 124–125
  middle-class Americans, 122–123, 161
  noise, 166, 166(n)
  of oceans, 73, 73(n), 111, 111(n)
  and overpopulation, 3, 117–121, 117(n),
    118(n), 120(n)
  particulate matter, 72, 72(n)
  penalties, 164
  percent produced by U.S., 3
  poor affected most, 122–123, 122(n)
  and power plants, 131

and Second Law of Thermodynamics,
    47, 48
  taxes, 165
  technology as cause, 118–121, 118(t),
    118(n), 119(t), 120(n)
  thermal, 129–132, 131(n)
Polychlorinated biphenyls (PCB's), 95
Poor:
  little impact on environment, 122–123
  and population growth, 122, 122(n),
    168
Population: (see also Population control,
    Population dynamics and Popula-
    tion growth)
  bomb, 6, 8, 9, 11
  crash, 36, 39
  defined, 61
  density, 33–34, 158, 162–163
  distribution, 162–163
    U.S., 34
  of earth, 1, 2, 6–10
  future projection, 2, 6–10
  implosion, 33–34 (see also Population
    density)
  maximum, 3, 38–40, 39(n), 39(f),
    132–133, 132(t), 133(n)
  optimum, 3, 38–40, 39(n), 39(f)
  U.S., 3, 9, 13, 19
  U.S. as percentage of world total, 2
  world, 1, 2
Population control, 25, 160–162
  absorption, 161
  attaining optimum population, 39–40
  China, 33(n)
  economic incentives, 162, 163
  effect of reducing birth rate, 136,
    137(f), 138(f), 139, 139(f), 140(f)
  family planning, 31, 161
  and foreign aid, 162
  freedom to have children, 40
  genocide issue, 168, 168(n)
  in India, 23
  involuntary methods, 162
  lack of government policies, 23–24, 25
  need to lower birth rates, 39–41
  new medical ethic, 161–162
  and poor, 122, 122(n), 168
  psychology of childbearing, 27, 27(n)
  remove tax deductions, 162
  sending people into space as a myth,
    112–113
  sterilization, 161
  war not a feasible method, 11(f), 12
Population dynamics, 16–41, 33(n)
  age structure, 17–24, 162
  birth rates, 16–17
  carrying capacity, 35–36, 35(f)
  cost of children, 26
  death rates, 16–17
  density of population, 33–34

difficulty with projecting future
change, 31
distribution of U.S. population, 33–34,
162–163
economic implications, 31, 31(n), 162,
168, 168(n)
in educational system, 161
fertility rate, 24–34
and immigration, 19, 19(n), 28, 31, 168
limits to growth, 35–41 (see also
S-curve)
major factors summarized, 33
maximum population, 38–40, 39(n),
39(f) 132–133, 132(t) (see also
S-curve)
mother's age at first child, 33(n)
number of children per family, 24–34
(see also Fertility rate)
number of children wanted, 31
optimum population, 38–40, 39(f), 39(n)
peak reproduction years in women,
20, 20(n), 21(f)
and per capita income, 31, 31(n)
and stationary state society, 31, 31(n),
32, 142, 142(n), 167–168
in Sweden, 32
Population growth:
age structure, 16–24
and agricultural revolution, 37(f), 37
birth rate, 16–17
and black Americans, 122, 122(n), 168
as a chain reaction, 11
and consumption, 12–13, 12(t), 117–121
cost of having children, 26, 26(t)
and DDT, 17
deaths from starvation and malnutrition, 40, 40(n)
death rate, 16–17
dependency load, 32
density, 34–5, 162–163
and disease, 41
doubling of, 2
doubling time, 10
economic implications, 31, 31(n), 32,
168(n), 169(n)
and fertility rate, 24–34
future, 2, 8(f), 25
and GNP, 12, 12(t)
history of, 37(f), 37–38
and hunger, 100–116
and immigration, 28, 31, 168
implications of, 11(t)
increase per day, 9
India, 9
and industrial revolution, 37–38
J-curve, 2, 3, 5, 6, 8(f)
limits of, 35–41 (see also S-curve)
and malnutrition, 2, 74, 105–107 (see
also Protein)

maximum population, 35–41, 39(f),
39(n), 132–133, 132(t), 133(n) (see
also Carrying capacity and
S-curve)
Mexico, 24
mother's age at first child, 33(n)
number of children wanted, 31
optimum population, 38–40, 39(f), 39(n)
past, 8(f)
and per capita income, 31, 31(n)
and pollution, 12–13, 12(t), 117–121,
117(n), 118(n), 118(t), 119(t), 120(n)
and poor, 122, 122(n), 168
projecting future change, 16–41, 24(n)
quality of parenthood, 26
rate of, 9
and sending people into space, 113
in suburbs, 34
throughout history, 10
and urbanization, 33–34
in U.S., 9, 12, 12(t), 13, 20, 28, 28(t)
and wars, 11(t), 12
Population Reference Bureau, 5(n), 9(n),
23(t), 27(n), 29(n)
Positive feedback, 84 (see also Cybernetics)
Potential energy, 43
Potter, N., 121(n)
Power plants: (see also Energy crisis)
breeder, 129
nuclear, 129–131, 130(n), 131(f)
thermal pollution, 129–132, 131(f),
131(n)
Power, cost of, 167
Predator control, side effects of, 92
Preservation of species, 87–92
Producers, 63–64 (see also Ecosystem)
Productivity of ecosystems, 110(n), 110
Protein:
consumption by pets, 106, 161
exploitation of underdeveloped
countries, 106–107, 106(n)
and hunger, 74
shortage of, 105–106, 105(n), 106(n)
South American fish to U.S., 106,
106(n)
Proverbs, 174
Psychology of childbearing, 27, 27(n)
Pyramid:
of energy, 101–102, 102(f), 104–105
of numbers, 101–102, 102(f), 104–105,
104(f)

Quality of life, 3, 6, 14
Randomness (see Disorder)
Raw materials, 107
Recycling, 160, 164
aluminum, 164
economics of, 126
paper, 164
required on most products, 167

Reich, Charles A., 148–149, 148(n)
Reimer, T., 79(n)
Resources, 125–133, 128(t)
　depletion of, 5, 127
　nonrenewable, 125–133
　reducing use of, 135, 136(f), 136, 138(f), 139, 139(f), 140(f), 166
　recycling of, 2
　use of by developed countries, 1, 2, 3, 117, 117(n)
　use by U.S., 3, 121–122, 121(n)
Respiration, and carbon cycles, 69, 69(n)
Rienow, Leona, 108, 108(n)
Rienow, Robert, 108, 108(n)
Ritchie-Calder, Lord, 129, 129(n)
Rose, D. J., 130(n)
Runoff of fertilizer, 75–82 (see also Nitrogen cycle)
Russia, arms race, 1
Ryan, W., 122(n)

Schaeffer, Francis A., 153(n)
Schistosomiasis, 89–90
Scientific laws, 42–43
S-curve, 35–41
　and carrying capacity, 35, 35(f), 36
　defined, 35, 35(f)
　homeostatic plateau, 35(f), 36
　meaning of, 36(n)–37(n)
Seaborg, Glenn T., 126(n)
Second Law of Thermodynamics, 45–51
　(see also Thermodynamics)
　and agriculture, 107–116
　apparent violations, 48–49
　can't be repealed, 55, 56
　and death, 48
　and degradation of energy, 50
　and disorder, 46–51
　and ecological crisis, 49–55, 147
　and energy degradation in an ecosystem, 64–66, 100–104
　and energy flow in an ecosystem, 64, 66–67, 69–72, 100–104
　and entropy, 49
　and environment, 49–55
　and food chains, 100–102, 101(n), 101(f), 102(f), 104–105, 104(f)
　and food from ocean, 110
　and growing food, 107–116
　and heat in environment, 50, 66–67, 71–72, 130–132
　and living organisms, 47–48
　and photosynthesis, 48
　and pollution, 47, 48
　significance of, 49–50, 54–55
　and solar energy, 48
　and synthetic food, 111
　and technological optimists, 107–116
　why we ignore it, 55
Senghaas, D., 156(n)
Seskin, E. B., 166(n)

Sewage treatment, as a cause of eutrophication, 78(n), 78(f), 79, 81–82, 81(f)
Shaw, George B., 172
Singer, S. F., 72(n), 77(n), 131(n)
Snail fever (see Schistosomiasis)
Snow, Sir C. P., 45
Social change, stages of, 150
Social costs, 165–166, 166(n), 168 (see also Economics)
Socolow, R. H., 131(n), 142(n), 169(n)
Soil:
　humus, 75–76
　loss of topsoil, 76
　nitrogen content, 75
Solar energy, 57–59
　amount reaching earth, 58
　disruption of flow into earth's atmosphere, 66–68, 71–72
　and ecosystems, 63–66, 65(f)
　nuclear fusion in sun, 48, 57
　and Second Law of Thermodynamics, 48
　use of, 130
Southeast Asia, oil resources, 128(n)
Spaceship (see Spaceship Earth)
Spaceship Earth, 5 (see also Earth)
　arrogant use of the term, 51–53, 156
　as a closed system, 51–52
　rules for living on, 13
　in trouble, 6
Spaceship Earth program, 155–157
Space program, 41
　as solution to population problem, 112–113
　spaceships as closed systems, 51–53
　value of, 113
Species, 1, 87–92
Spengler, Joseph J., 142(n), 169(n)
Spontaneous processes, 45–51 (see als Thermodynamics)
SST, 164
Stability: (see also Ecosystem)
　in ecosystems, 83, 87, 96, 96(n)
Stamler, P. S., 12(n), 119(t), 120(n)
Starvation, 2, 40, 40(n), 105, 105(n)
Stationary state society: (see also Zero population growth)
　advantages of, 31, 164(n), 169(n)
　age structure of, 32, 32(t)
Steady state, 52 (see also Stationary state)
　economics, 142, 142(n), 167–169, 168(n), 169(n)
　in ecosystem, 66, 83
Steam engine, efficiency of, 54, 130
Sterilization, 161 (see also Population control)
Strip mines, 108, 108(n)
Structure of ecosystems, 63–66, 65(f) (see also Ecosystem)

Stycos, J. M., 150
Sulfur dioxide, 80–81 (see also Air pollution)
Sun (see Solar energy)
Sweden, and zero population growth, 32
Sylvatic plague, 90
Synergy, 85–86 (see also Cybernetics)
Synthetic food, 45, 111 (see also Food)
System(s): (see also Thermodynamics)
  closed, 5, 49, 51–52
  open, 51–53

Tamplin, A. R., 126(n)
Taxes on pets, 161
Technological optimism, 3, 146
Technological optimists, 107
Technology:
  as cause of pollution, 118–121, 118(t), 118(n), 119(t), 120(n)
  danger of neo-Luddite revolution, 154, 154(n)
  evaluation of, 166–167
  and overpopulation, 118–121, 118(n), 118(t), 119(t), 120(n)
  and pollution, 118–121, 118(t), 119(t), 120(n)
  unwise use of, 158
Temperature, 44, 44(n)
Temperature control in living organisms, 84 (see also Cybernetics)
Terry, Mark, 171(n)
Theobald, Robert, 168(n)
Thermal pollution, 129–132, 131(n)
Thermodynamic efficiency, 130
Thermodynamic revolution, 133–134
Thermodynamics, 42–56
  and agriculture, 45, 48, 107–116
  closed systems, 51–53
  and death, 48
  and disorder, 46–51
  and ecological crisis, 49–55, 173
  efficiency, 54
  and energy crisis, 130
  and energy flow in an ecosystem, 64, 66–67, 69–72, 100–104
  and entropy, 49–51
  and environment, 49, 113–116
  first law of, 43–45
  and food chains, 100–102, 101(n), 101(f), 104–105, 104(f)
  and food from oceans, 110
  and growing food, 107–116
  and living organisms, 47–48
  nonspontaneous processes, 45–46
  open systems, 51–53
  and order, 46–51
  and photosynthesis, 48
  and pollution, 47, 48
  Second Law of, 45–51 (see also Second Law of Thermodynamics)

and solar energy, 48
spontaneous processes, 45–51
and steady state, 52
surroundings, 43
and synthetic foods, 45, 111
system, 43, 47
and use of resources, 126, 131, 133–134
Thermostat, 83–84 (see also Cybernetics)
Thompson, W. S., 33(n)
Thoreau, Henry D., 15
Tin, supply of, 128(t)
Toffler, Alvin, 14, 14(n)
Topsoil, loss of in U.S., 76, 108
Tragedy of the commons, 155, 155(n)
Trophic levels, 66 (see also Ecosystem and Food Chain)
Tschirley, F. H., 92(n)
Turkey, population growth problems, 34

Udall, Stewart E., 123
Underdeveloped countries:
  age structure, 21, 22(f), 23(t)
  birth rate, 18(f)
  children per family, 23–24
  consequences of development, 133–134
  death rates, 18(f)
  foreign aid, 162
  likelihood of development, 133–134
  no hope, 143
  overpopulatoin in, 3, 18–19, 21–25, 34, 40–41, 117
  protein exploitaton of, 106, 106(n)
  urbanization of, 34
United Nations hunger estimates, 9, 10, 115, 115(f)
United States:
  age structure of population, 32, 32(t), 162
  arms race, 1, 169
  birth rate, 18–19, 20–21
  consumption in, 3, 117–123
  cost of having children, 26, 26(t)
  death rate, 19
  diet, 105, 106
  energy consumption, 127, 127(n)
  farm population, 34
  fertility rates, 27, 27(t)
  future population growth, 20, 27, 28(t), 28, 29
  garbage costs, 166
  growth of suburbs, 34
  immigration, 19, 19(n), 28, 31, 161
  increase in fertilizer production, 76
  increase in pollution, 12, 12(t), 117–123
  loss of topsoil, 108
  miltary expenditures, 169
  population 3, 19, 121–123
  population commission, 26, 26(n)
  population as percentage of world population, 2

population density, 33
population distribution, 34, 162–163
population growth, 9, 13, 19
rate of urbanization of land, 107–108
urban problems, 33
use of resources, 1, 2, 3, 121–122, 121(n)
water use, 109
zero population growth, 28–31
zero population growth as national policy, 161
United States Bureau of Mines, 128
United States Department of Health, Education and Welfare, 123
Uranium, supply of, 128(t), 129
Urban crisis, 34 (see also Population density)
Urbanization, 33–34
U.S.S.R. (see Russia)

Values and ecological crisis, 51–55, 143
Van Tassel, A. J., 118(n)
Viet Nam, ecological effects of herbicides, 92–93, 92(n)

Wagar, J. A., 142(n)
War, 12
death rate from, 11, 11(t)
and population growth, 11, 11(t), 12
Water: (see also Water pollution)
desalination, 109
and growing food, 108–109, 109(n)
inadequate supply, 2
raise cost of, 167
supply of, 10, 108–109, 108(n)
use in U.S., 108–109

Water pollution:
from animal wastes, 75–82, 78(f), 81(f)
from automobile exhausts, 78(f), 79, 81, 81(f)
from feedlots, 75–82, 78(f), 81(f)
fertilizer, 75–82, 78(f), 81(f)
from nitrates, 75–82
from sewage treatment plants, 78, 78(f), 79, 81–82, 81(f)
Westinghouse, desalination, 109
Wharton, C. R., Jr., 114(n)
Whitehead, Alfred N., 159
White, Lynn, Jr., 153(n)
Whittaker, Robert, 73(n)
Wilderness, preservation of, 99
Wildlife, preservation of, 99
Wilson, McLandburgh, 146
World Future Society, 34(n), 89(f)
World Health Organization, 90, 166, 166(n)
World models, 134–143 (see Cybernetics)
Wright, R. T., 153(n)

Zero population growth (ZPG), 35, 36
and age structure, 32, 32(t)
and carrying capacity, 35, 35(f), 36
economic implications, 31, 31(n), 32, 168, 169
as goal for U.S., 31
implications of, 28–29
and per capita income, 31, 31(n)
and Sweden, 32
in U.S., 28–31
as U.S. policy, 161
Zinc, supply of, 128(t)
ZPG (see Zero Population Growth)